GIACOMO LEOPARDI

SELECTED POEMS

(ITALIAN TEXT INCLUDED)

WITH EXCERPTS FROM THE POET'S JOURNALS, LETTERS, AND NOTES

TRANSLATED BY

THOMAS G. BERGIN

AND

ANNE PAOLUCCI

EDITED, WITH AN INTRODUCTION, BY

ANNE PAOLUCCI

Library of Congress Cataloging in Processing Data

Leopardi, Giacomo, 1798-1837.
   [Poems. English & Italian. Selections]
   Selected poems of Giacomo Leopardi : (Italian text
included) and some prose excerpts from the poet's
journals, letters, and notes (in English) / translated by
Thomas G. Bergin and Anne Paolucci ; edited
with an introduction by Anne Paolucci.
      p. cm.
   English and Italian.
   ISBN 1-932107-05-3 (alk. paper)
   1. Leopardi, Giacomo, 1798-1837 – Translations into
English. I. Bergin, Thomas Goddard, 1904-1987.
II. Paolucci, Anne. III. Title.

PQ4709.E5A1 2003
851'.7–dc21
                                        2003051191

Published for
THE BAGEHOT COUNCIL
by
GRIFFON HOUSE PUBLICATIONS
P. O. Box 468
Smyrna Delaware 19977

CONTENTS

This book has been made possible by grants from

THE NEW YORK STATE SENATE
and
THE ITALIAN MINISTRY OF FOREIGN AFFAIRS

INTRODUCTION

Leopardi stands alone as the great modern poet of Italy;[1] in the wider spectrum of Italian literature, he is second only to Dante; and, in the judgment of most critics,

rivaling Petrarch in the musicality of his melancholic songs of love and death, matching Alfieri in the austerity of his pessimistic passion, and approaching Dante in his capacity to give poetic expression to a most powerfully experienced sense of an entire universe, in his case a godless universe sublimely devoid of meaning. Leopardi is, besides, virtually without a rival in his mastery of philosophic and satiric dialogue and expository prose.[2]

His wide-ranging talent — poet, satirist, scholar, and prose writer — is buttressed by an unusual preparation as a voracious and eclectic reader in at least five languages and long and concentrated study of Greek and Latin philology. His study of Greek texts prompted him, while still very young, to write poems in the manner of his favorite Greek authors — poems which Greek scholars mistook for authentic Greek originals.

He was familiar with some modern philosophical works[3] and at one point annnounced his "conversion" to philosophy, a claim which Giovanni Gentile — the most prominent Hegelian philosopher and literary critic of the twentieth century, friend and colleague of Benedetto Croce — dismisses, pointing out that Leopardi never approached philosophy as a systematic, formal study of the subject but as a personal exploration for answers to the large questions that plagued him: the meaning of life and death, the place and role of man on earth, the nature of fate and the universe, retaining only what appealed to him, what served his purpose as a writer and as a human being.

Those questions are the major subject of his poems and find eloquent expression in them;[4] they are also the burden of his letters, notebooks, journals, and diaries, in which he scrutinizes and analyzes his thoughts and records his impressions and reflections as they occur, on a daily basis. And for this reason also, Gentile notes, these daily philosophical observations do not constitute a *philosophy*; they are true for one day, not necessarily for another.[5] As a philosopher, Gentile makes clear, Leopardi was at best mediocre.[6]

And yet, in seeking his own personal answers, in trying to give meaning to his life and his world and in trying to hold his experiences together in a meaningful way, philosophizing, in other words, in a personal context, Leopardi emerges as "exquisitely" philosophical, a poet who could reach into the most sensitive areas of the soul and strike deep familiar chords with his questioning, his pain, his uncertainties, his "philosophy" of life as he saw it and described it.[7]

That probing is the life and soul of Leopardi's world of poetry, a universe where the answers to the large questions about life and death, nature, the soul, fate, history, progress, are pretty grim. Man's life is an exercise in futility; his legacy, one of suffering without respite, resignation without rewards. Fate is a cruel step-mother who has no comfort to offer. Life is a rushing toward oblivion; in the end, a blessed release. Suicide, in fact, is a constant temptation, death a recurring theme.

In depicting a godless universe in which man plays a meaningless role, Leopardi seems to distance himself from other Romantic poets who saw in the return to nature, in the pursuit of ideal Love, in the inspiration of ancient Greece, a new and better future and subjects for a renewed poetic world. For Leopardi, those same Romantic ideals and hopes were cause for grief. Nature may be the handmaiden of God, as Wordsworth describes her, but for Leopardi she is the indifferent force that can destroy in a matter of seconds entire cities and all inside them. Nature brings death and destruction with floods and famines, levels whole areas with earthquakes, buries houses, people, and fields under the boiling flow of Vesuvius. The silent emptiness of the universe is awesome only in its purposeless vastness. Even the beauty of ancient Greece and the grandeur of imperial Rome are reminders of nature's erosion of entire civilizations through time. Understandably, many critics have labeled Leopardi a *pessimist.*[8]

Such a view rests on a seemingly solid foundation; but a closer look at his purposeless universe, his indifferent world, reveals a paradoxical attitude. Though expressed in strong and often satiric words, at times betraying anger and rage even, Leopardi's "pessimism" is more often than not balanced by a state of soul that betrays pity, yearning, a tenderness toward the world and his fellow men. He thunders against the fools who would like to change the world, who exalt man as the major player in a universe created expressly for his pleasure and gain, who believe in a glowing future. At the same time, his heart is touched by these errors, these false illusions, and he responds to them with pity and sympathy. He is moved by the brief happy season of youth, gone all too soon; by the suffering we all must endure; even by something as seemingly trivial as the reflective sadness that settles over us when the day of rest, our Sunday or holiday, so full of promise the night before, so eagerly anticipated in the morning, comes to an end. His attachments are real and often simple ones; his spirit reaches out to others who have not yet realized the grim reality of life, who are still able to enjoy their brief hours of contentment and joy. He envies them but without resentment, recognizing the bleak future in store for them, anticipating what they must face and accept, eventually. In retrospect, he describes lovingly the little maid who sings at the loom, unaware of how soon she will be thrust into the eternal darkness of an early grave. He watches the hard-working farmer, the wandering shepherd, the laborer, living out their tedious days, all busy plodding through their daily routines and thus keeping the hard truths about life and death at a distance. He himself yearns for oblivion, for death, equates it with love, lingers over suicide, but in the end, like Hamlet, turns back to brood about the large unanswered questions that give us pause. Even on the subject of progress and the potential of man, his scorn is directed toward the glib and ignorant prophets of the future rather than the idea itself.

The tender feelings, the poignant emotional uncertainties and often contradictory attitudes expressed in both his poetry and prose, suggest that the label of "pessimist," so often used to describe Leopardi, may in fact be inadequate, misleading even. Some critics have, in fact, gone to the other extreme, insisting that Leopardi is basically an *optimist*.[9] Gentile himself subscribes in part to such a view. For him, Leopardi's love of virtue, his faith in the potential of the human spirit, in the illusions which even nature cannot wholly destroy in us, spring from an intuitive spirituality which preserves and exalts that very world the poet seems to undermine and reject. His view of life, nature, the world, mankind, love, rests in fact on contradictions. In a way, he himself is a paradox.

> Although he is the most purely romantic personality Italian culture can boast of, Leopardi was at the same time thoroughly classical in his approach to literature, and, in that sense, antiromantic.[10]

And, more specifically, his approach to poetry reflects a pessimism less explicit than many critics have suggested. For starters, mastery of one's craft is the result of a commitment to excel; it demands a conscious effort to learn the basic rules, to practice the craft, to seek one's own style. All of which is the result of a positive and irresistible urge to share one's thoughts and feelings in writing, with others. To feel the oppression of life is one thing; to stand back and survey it in order to communicate it is something quite different.

Gentile insists that Leopardi's energetic assertion of man's dark destiny is something *positive*. To be able to stand back and survey the empty fate of humanity is an exercise in which distance brings illumination, precision, a kind of relief, a deliberate effort to communicate and convince. To find the proper words for such views, to find analogies that are immediate and convincing and real, to communicate all this adequately requires a state of soul that is something other than sheer apathy and despair. Of course, all this is true of poets and writers everywhere, of anyone who tries to express his feelings and thoughts, whether dark and oppressive, or hopeful and secure in faith and certainty. The act of writing is by its very nature a *positive assertion*.

In that sense, Leopardi surely was asserting his power as a poet in the care he took with his writing: molding a poetic language of his own, a language that is deceptively simple but often complex; choosing words with meticulous care; consciously exercising his mastery of poetic forms; using syntax in unusual ways to serve his special needs. His mastery of poetic structure, his extraordinary philological training, his humor — even when bitter and sarcastic — suggest an awareness on the poet's part of the importance of skill and an unflagging commitment to his art, a conscious purpose to excel, which surely mitigates, to some degree, even the most oppressive despair. One might also cite on this side of the argument the poet's fervent desire for fame and glory, a hope often mentioned in his poems and prose writings, ostensibly abandoned at a certain age but probably never wholly relinquished.

Even as he undermines the illusions we create for ourselves, Leopardi reminds us, paradoxically, of the need for them: one simply cannot live out this life without the relief they offer. His own bitter experience with love, the most beguiling illusion of all, did not destroy in him the yearning for it. In poems like "Alla sua donna" (a hymn to

ix

ideal beauty) he confesses that he will be more than satisfied with an "approximation," a "likeness" in the flesh, since the ideal will never be accessible to us in this life. The eminent literary critic and historian, Francesco De Sanctis, calls attention to this dialectic spiraling from despair to hope, observing with his usual keen insight that Leopardi makes you long for the very things he seems to reject, makes you love the things he dismisses, makes you yearn for the illusions he has abandoned.[11]

In fact, he clings to many illusions even as he dismisses them, and he often finds large consolation in having been able to overcome most of the temptations of life. In the end, however, he emerges as the most bitter poet of Italian literature, the isolated voice — if not of pessimism as such — of romantic disillusionment, matched only in English literature by that extraordinary exception to the atheistic pragmatism and agnosticism of his age, James Thomson. Thomson's *The City of Dreadful Night* is indeed, as one critic has noted, the most pessimistic poem in any language, a modern Dantesque journey through a world of night, without hope or love or faith, a nineteenth-century hell on earth. Thomson knew Italian well, and not just Dante: he had translated Leopardi's *Operette morali* and other pieces, and cited both poets on the dedicatory page of the *City*. If not himself a true pessimist, Leopardi certainly inspired the greatest pessimist poet of England.

For Thomson too, that small glimmer of hope that is human love, what Matthew Arnold eloquently describes in "Dover Beach," was denied him. Thomson devotes an entire canto in his *City* to the death of his beloved, his last illusion shattered; Leopardi describes in several places his infatuation with Fanny Targioni Tozzetti, the one woman he claimed to have loved deeply. His ambiguous feelings toward her — the confounding of a disappointing reality with an indestructible Ideal whose embodiment always falls short of perfection — are recalled with bitter-sweet intensity in "Aspasia" (1834), where the "accomplished temptress" is given the name of the noted courtesan and described in less than flattering terms for, in his opinion, leading him on. In spite of his bitter show of sarcastic detachment, the experience brought him to the edge of despair. He falls back, as on other occasions, to contemplating the perfect but unattainable Ideal, a favorite and recurring theme that sustained him throughout his brief life and is explored in poems like "Alla sua donna."

For Leopardi, the gloom of life was intensified by his solitary existence in the palatial residence of his parents in Recanati, a provincial town in the Marche region, where he was born in 1798. When he was twenty-one, he tried to escape from his father's house but failed in his effort. It wasn't until April 1830, at the age of thirty-two, that he finally left Recanati, never to return. In Rome, Florence, Bologna, Naples, and other literary and cultural centers, he stayed with friends like Antonio Ranieri and his uncle Carlo Antici. He was a frequent guest at the gatherings of Vieusseux and met many important people of the time, such as Pietro Brighenti, Count Carlo Pepoli, the erudite scholar Luigi De Sinner, the historian-general Pietro Colletta, the publisher Fortunato Stella, the well-known novelist Alessandro Manzoni, and the patriot Gioberti, at the same time strengthening already existing ties with friends like Pietro Giordani. The poet was only thirty-nine years old when he died on June 14, 1837 in Naples, while a guest in the home of Antonio Ranieri.

There are all kinds of translations. Dante Gabriel Rossetti's English versions of the *stilnovists* enjoyed a large readership for many years, perhaps because they bore the unmistakable and familiar mark, popular at that time, of the English poet's own style and musical cadences. They served an important purpose too, in that his was the only large effort to make available the poets of Dante's early period, including Dante himself. But when Ezra Pound some decades later published his translations of the poems of Dante's close friend and fellow-poet, Guido Cavalcanti, including many that had been rendered into English earlier by Rossetti, critical readers soon became aware of how much of the original Rossetti had lost in translation. Pound's version had its own indelible and unmistakable signature, of course, with all its familiar eccentricities and exaggerations; but on the whole it remained true to the consistency and the cumulative effect of the Italian, especially Cavalcanti's tight organic structuring of images around a central core — easy enough to miss or ignore, as Rossetti often did. The superficial fluency of Rossetti's versions ultimately was misleading; Pound chose to maintain, among other things, the architectural precision, the image clusters of the originals, at times using words in unusual ways to get as close to the original as possible.[12] Both were poets, both had the ear necessary to produce a fair translation, but Pound seems to have had a keener perception of Cavalcanti's deft handling of image clusters, so vital in *stilnovist* poetry.

In the introduction to his slim volume, Pound admits the frustrations he encountered along the way and the slow stages by which he moved from a commentary on the poems (explaining that it would be impossible ever to reproduce the special quality of the Italian) to paraphrasing each poem, and, finally, unable to resist the urge to try his poet's skill at it, succumbing to a full translation.

I found in Leopardi's case, similar and equally frustrating difficulties. His style is terse, limpid, clipped, deceptively simple; the ironic turns are dramatically abrupt and emotionally jarring. The philologist and linguist, the scholar, the sensitive but isolated human being, jostle one another in his poetry. And like Dante and Coleridge — who taught us the paradox of expressing the inexpressible — Leopardi proves himself a perfectionist in the care taken to describe in a new poetic tongue his inspired vision of life as a meaningless burden.

In a way reminiscent of the *stilnovists* and Dante himself, Leopardi often described and expanded on the physiological and psychological effects that even the most ordinary occurrences can produce in a sensitive and discerning individual. An empty expanse of countryside, interrupted by a hedge, suddenly becomes mysterious and suggestive; sounds reaching the ear indistinctly, as though from a great distance, are especially appealing, precisely because of their vagueness. Poems like "L'infinito" and "Alla luna," remind us that many things that we take for granted, familiar sights and experiences, can be transformed into something new and mysterious. The most ordinary descriptions, the most commonplace experience in Leopardi's poetry become infinitely suggestive. We are also reminded of what stunning experiments in poetic form such poems represent: the apparent simplicity of "L'infinito," for example, is actually a stunning masterpiece of fifteen unrhymed hendecasyllables.

His observations, noted in detail in his letters, journals, the *Zibaldone, Scritti vari,* etc. (some excerpts from these sources have been included in the present volume) are indicators of just how intense this scrutiny was, how seriously the poet considered it, how carefully he detailed his analysis of even the most ordinary events, familiar sights and emotions, especially love. All this, when converted into poetry may seem casual at first; but Leopardi is anything but casual. He forces us into a new alertness, opens our eyes to the obvious, clears out our ears so that we can hear things in a new way — always in a style that is inviting in its ultimate simplicity, but also, always — as one critic describes it — *austere*. He beguiles us into thinking he is easy to grasp, his words simple, his thoughts familiar; but as we go on we realize that his words mean more than we thought, his descriptions carefully set up to produce resonances not recognizable at first, his easy-sounding vocabulary the source of correspondences that a casual reading may well miss.

I came to appreciate Leopardi in these and many other ways when, almost two decades ago, I undertook with my friend and Renaissance colleague, Thomas Bergin of Yale University, to translate into English some of Leopardi's poems. Our joint venture came about as a result of a friendship which grew out of our meeting in May 1974, during a week-long convention in Washington D.C., marking the 600th anniversary of Petrarch's death. As the best-known translator and scholar of early Renaissance Italian authors, Tom was featured on a number of programs, including one where I had been invited to present a paper. It was my only meeting with Professor Bergin, Sterling Professor at Yale, but we soon started to correspond and phoned one another often.

It was during one of our phone conversations that the idea for this book first came up. We had got on to the subject of translation, and as we exchanged views on that all-important but often thankless task, I happened to mention that I had tried my hand at translating a number of Leopardi's poems over the years, had even published several, here and there, but was never satisfied. I would pull out the "work-in-progress" from time to time, spend a number of hours revising this or that poem, then — utterly drained by the effort — put everything back in desk drawers until the next time. I complained that translating Machiavelli's *Mandragola,* short stories and other prose of Pirandello, even my brief forays into Dante, had not posed the same difficulties I encountered with Leopardi. Tom listened and then confessed that he too had a number of translations of Leopardi's poems tucked away in desk drawers, he too kept returning to them, never fully satisfied, although he too had published a number of them in scattered journals and anthologies. At one point in the exchange, we both reached the same conclusion: why not work together to get out a small volume?

We were both enthusiastic about the idea, but in his characteristically gentlemanly way, Tom left it for me to start things moving. When I got back to him, several months later, he confessed that he had been waiting for me to send him some preliminary materials but had not wished to burden me with a promise I might not be able to fulfill in the light of many other obligations and commitments. We began to work at the translations at an almost feverish pace, late in 1985.

The first thing we did was exchange what we had on hand, those translations each of us had worked on separately. Then we agreed on a tentative list of poems that should be included in the collection. We decided we should take on not only the more familiar poems but some of the more difficult ones like "Bruto minore," "La ginestra" and "Aspasia," the bane of many translators who have tried their hand at them. I suggested we include some of Leopardi's commentaries on the poems (I had already translated a number of them), but Tom expressed concern that these would make the book inordinately large. For the same reason, we agreed, at the time, that the Italian originals should not be included.

We exchanged, revised, commented on the translations by letter and phone for almost an entire year. The task was frustrating for reasons already mentioned. Even for Tom, who had tackled Dante, Boccaccio, Petrarch, Vico, and early French poets, among others, and had won wide acclaim for his work, Leopardi presented a formidable challenge. In a letter to me, dated January 28. 1986, he commented about our first joint effort, "L'infinito" (at first glance, one of the "easier" poems):

> It was probably a mistake to begin with this one — it is, as you know, very tight and compacted. Even with your version and my school text original (very heavily glossed and frequently paraphrased) I found it very hard work. What I was after here was to preserve the meter . . . and keep the meaning honest — not always literal but at least saying what L. is saying. And of course I agree that a

translation should not sound like a translation. Often, however, L.'s language is faintly archaic and a good translation is bound to mirror that.

He recognized, as Ezra Pound had recognized in his efforts to translate Guido Cavalcanti's tight clusters of interwoven images (respecting the *stilnovist* insistence on giving the most ordinary words special and precise meanings), that even the shortest and seemingly simplest work by a gifted poet who shapes the language into new and surprising patterns presents the translator, in addition to and apart from all else, with an intricate puzzle.

The difficulties mentioned, however, did not dampen our efforts in the least. Tom worked uninterruptedly, in spite of failing health. In October, 1986, I suggested we might consider bringing the project to a close before the end of the year, and that I would then review all the materials, prepare and edit the manuscript, and submit it for publication. But when Tom died, a year later, the work was once more laid aside in the crush of other more immediate commitments.

When I pulled out the manuscript, early in 2002, I excused my delay with the reminder that time always sharpens the focus and refines the critical judgment. The break, in fact, made me appreciate Tom's efforts at searching for the right "voice" and meaning. I found, also, that at this distance I was able to see the whole with greater clarity and therefore could make consistent decisions as to the final disposition and language of its parts — the final assignment entrusted to me. Still, there were many things that needed to be reviewed and revised if the translations were to be both readable and accurate. So I pushed everything else aside and gave myself to the task.

I found that in quite a few instances both Tom and I had been misled by the incredibly flexible but often ambiguous syntax; that Italian word endings often had to be re-examined carefully as a clue to adjective-noun relationships and therefore to meaning; that the terse construction characteristic of Leopardi was easily lost in trying to maintain the original meter in English, and that perhaps it would be best to retain Leopardi's tight, often abrupt transitions, after all. In short, I found myself returning to the Italian text and working directly from it once again, then comparing the current versions with both my earlier ones and Tom's.

My main consideration was to maintain, as closely as possible, Leopardi's language, and avoid all extraneous words. No effort was made to retain rhyming lines or, as in the case of poems like "Primo amore" ("First Love"), the difficult *terza rima*. I also tried, wherever possible, to keep adjectives as adjectives, nouns as nouns, participial and other phrases as they appear in the Italian; to retain correspondences, repetitions, and quick inversions, in order to maintain the precision of meaning and give words and phrases the weight they carried in the original.

It was my decision to include a sampling of excerpts from Leopardi's notes, journals, and letters, where the poet comments on matters contained in the poems. I also brought together some early notebook entries (1820) as a brief introduction, in the poet's own words, to some of the recurring ideas which continued to occupy his mind and his poetic fantasy for many years. There was no time for Tom to deal with these, nor did he get around to considering the *Dialogo di Federico Ruysch e delle sue mummie* (the only piece drawn from the *Operette morali*), which is in a totally different style and mood from those of the *Canti* and provides an excellent example of Leopardi's sharp wit and humor. After careful deliberation, I also decided to reverse our earlier decision and included the Italian text for each of the poems.

In the end I had to ask myself: how much of all these efforts to make Leopardi accessible in English will get through in translation? Not the fragile lyric quality of the original, with all its native resonances. But something of his style survives translation, as well as a great deal of his thought, the intensity with which he approached life and looked upon the world; the attention given to the most ordinary occurrences, teaching us to see the things around us with a clearer vision. He instructs us in dealing with love and death, the two emotions around which our conscious lives circle; and he holds up, for us to see, what he believes to be the truth about nature, the great deceiver, laying before us at the same time all its attractive manifestations — the woods, hills, streams, the open sky, the waning day, dusk, the moon, night, the clouds, the stars, other galaxies, infinite silent spaces beyond the earth. He depicts death as a welcome lover, love as a potential death; all the while fixing forever in our imagination his own vivid experiences of the simple life around him: the calm after a storm, Sunday in the village, the young maid who died before reaching adulthood, all poignantly recalled in his heart, in his empty hope, in his *noia*, the *ennui* we humans are all prone to.

Noia. One of Leopardi's favorite words. How does one translate it? The dictionaries define it as "boredom," "tedium," "*ennui*," but none of these words are adequate equivalents for what Leopardi had in mind. For him the word suggests restlessness and a profound apathy at the same time, or, as one critic tries to explain it, "physically a state produced by the gradually increasing arrest of the activity of the senses culminating in their all but complete paralysis, mentally a state appropriate to this, produced by a life of pure introspection culminating in apprehension of the ultimate truth that all is nothing, *i.e.* that the end of being is really non-being."[13] In Leopardi's own words:

> . . . what is meant by saying of a living person that at any moment when he is neither rejoicing nor suffering, he must perforce be a victim of *ennui*? We mean that he can never cease to desire happiness, that is, pleasure and enjoyment. This desire, when it is not satisfied nor on the

other hand directly opposed by that which is contrary to enjoyment, is *ennui*.[14]

No word or phrase in English conveys all that Leopardi pours into that one word *noia*. It contains the basic theme of Romantic restlessness. Byron, Keats, Shelley, Novalis, Hoerderlin, Heine, Musset, De Vigny, Hugo, in their best vein, wrote of little else. For Leopardi *noia* is also a reminder of the littleness, the nothingness of man, who in his constant yearning for the unknown, the impossible, the god-like, sometimes forgets the passage in *Ecclesiastes*: "What is man that thou are mindful of him?" For Leopardi *noia* is a tremendous longing to contract into nothing, frustrated by a million equally tremendous longings to expand into everything — so that when the expansion takes place it feels suddenly like contraction, while the contraction feels like expansion and vice versa — something like the dialectical spiraling of opposites, reminding us of Jimmy Durante's grostesque "did you ever have the feeling that you wanted to stay, together with the feeling that you wanted to go?" and the excruciating self-alienation on the Cross: "My God, my God, why hast thou forsaken me?" where "Thou" and "Me" are both somehow very God. In between is that agony we identify in our time with existentialism. It is essentially the Romantic agony. It says with horror, there is no God; and at the same time, that only God Himself could think so divine a thought. It's like an alternating current: the more he thinks himself nothing, the more man feels divine; and the more divine he feels, the more he knows himself to be nothing — like two empty mirrors reflecting into themselves, reproducing to infinity, divine-like infinity, their image of nothingness.

It was with this understanding of Leopardi's seemingly contradictory attitudes toward life and the world; of the illusion he produces, in his poetry, of spontaneity when in fact his language is the product of meticulous study and wide reading, perfected through long practice; of his insistence that the mark of all good poetry must always be *clearness* and *simplicity*,[15] that I took up these translations again. I soon discovered that having to decide on a final version in these terms was a much greater challenge than I had anticipated. I was often tempted to abandon the project: there were just too many problems. My worst moment was when I realized that I had spent two full days on six lines. My depression at that point was almost as heavy a burden as Leopardi's *noia*.

Of course, by then I was committed. Leopardi was an intimate voice, his effortless cadences and abrupt, often elliptical, constructions a perverse challenge. Somewhere along the line I reviewed my options and decided that my first priority should be to stay as close to the original as possible, to approximate that clearness and simplicity Leopardi insisted was basic to all good poetry — and which he stunningly achieved in his own work. As a corollary, and equally important, I felt I had to avoid the temptation of *interpreting* lines, which often meant lengthening them, and had to choose words that suggested something of the simple, lyrical beauty of the Italian without destroying the easy tone of the original. I avoided archaisms and tried, instead, for Leopardi's flowing, almost conversational tone. Most important, I felt I should respect his tight syntax, his abrupt transitions, and try to reproduce as closely as possible his simple but suggestive vocabulary. The task, as I saw it, was to prove as best I could that Leopardi is indeed a poet of the people, one who in Italy is not only taught in the schools but quoted often and lovingly by shopkeepers and housewives, students and scholars.

Although translations are never perfect and, as Tom himself would have agreed, never "finished" in any true sense, I am reasonably certain that he would have been pleased with this effort.

ANNE PAOLUCCI
New York, September, 2003

NOTES

[The Italian text used throughout is Giacomo Leopardi, Opere, a cura di Sergio Solmi *Milano/Napoli, Ricciardo Ricciardi, Ed.]*

1. Ugo Foscolo (1778-1827), whose *Last Letters of Jacopo Ortis* — inspired by Goethe's *Werther* — brought him international fame, is the only other Italian poet of the Romantic Age who demands attention; but his reputation rests on the one work mentioned, rather than on a body of works, and *Jacopo Ortis* survives today primarily as the expression of an important literary/historical turning point in Italian literature.

2. Anne and Henry Paolucci, "Leopardi," in *The Reader's Adviser* Vol. 2. 13th Edition. Maurice Charney, ed. (R. R. Bowker Company, New York & London, 1986), p. 322.

3. See *Opere complete di Giovanni Gentile. Manzoni e Leopardi.* G. Sansoni, Firenze, 1937, p. 46.

4. *Ibid.,* pp. 94ff. See also Gentile's eloquent description of poetry as the voice of the people, accessible to all (as opposed to the magnificent isolation of philosophy) and Leopardi as a poet who can touch the humblest of hearts. (p. 100)

5. ". . . è chiaro che, se in questi sette volumi [diaries] abbiamo, per dir così, i segreti documenti di tutto il lavorìo intimo di quello spirito, non potremo apparezzarli nel loro giusto valore, se prescindiamo dalle loro rispettive date; perchè a chi scrive ogni giorno le proprie riflessioni, la verità è quasi la verità di quel giorno: e quel lavoro di sistemazione e organizzazione, per cui di tutti i pensieri slegati si possa fare un tutto coerente, manca." *Ibid.,* p. 36.

6. *Ibid.,* p. 46.

7. *Ibid.,* pp. 94ff.

8. See Gentile's excellent review of the critics. *Ibid.,* pp. 33-83.

9. *Ibid.,* p. 75.

10.. Anne and Henry Paolucci, p. 322.

11. "Leopardi . . . non crede al progress, e te lo fa desiderare: non crede alla libertà, e te la fa amare. Chiama illusioni l'amore, la gloria, la virtù, e te ne accende in petto un desiderio inesausto." *Gentile,* pp. 50ff.

12. *E.g.* Pound translates the first line of one of the poems, "Avete in voi i fiori e la verdura," as "You have in you the flowers and the green," using the word green as a substantive to approximate the substantive use of "verdura" in the Italian ("green things," "verdant growth").

13. See Geoffrey L. Bickersteth, *The Poems of Leopardi, edited with an Introduction and Notes and a Verse Translation in the Metres of the Original* (Russell & Russell, New York, 1923, 1973), p. 99.

14. *Ibid.,* p. 101.

15. See Bickersteth, "Chapter II. The Poet's Art" (pp. 44-89), which opens with these words: "It may be safely asserted that no poet in the literature of the world has ever devoted more time and thought than did Leopardi to investigating and defining the principles that should govern poetic composition, or been more learned that he was in all that appertains to the art of poetry as practised in every age and tongue." (p. 44)

BRIEF CHRONOLOGY

1798 (June 29). Born in Recanati to Count Monaldo and Adelaide Antici.

1808. Still under the guidance of his Jesuit tutor, Sanchini (who will continue in that role until 1812), Leopardi begins his long stretch of independent study in the Recanati palace library, "mad and utterly desperate," during which time he will master not only Greek, but also Hebrew, English, French, and Spanish.

1811-1812. Translates Horace's *Arte poetica*, writes some playful poems, and sketches out a tragedy, *Pompeo in Egitto*.

1813. Compiles *Storia dell'astronomia*.

1814-1815. Produces translations, with commentaries, of Greek and Latin writers of the "decadence" (rhetoricians and Church Fathers of the II century).

1815. Writes *Saggio sopra gli errori popolari degli antichi*, translates Mosco and the *Batracomiomachia*, which he will later revise in two successive versions.

1816. Acknowledges what he will later call his "literary conversion," turning to Italian letters and poetry. Translates Homer and Virgil and publishes an imaginary version of an alleged *Inno a Nettuno*. Suffers the first serious incident of ill-health, brought on in an already weak constitution by the many hours spent in research and study. Writes during this time his first "original" poem, "Appressamento della morte." Continues his philological studies on Frontone, on Hebrew texts, the reputation of Horace among the ancients, etc.

1817. Begins a correspondence with the classicist and patriot, Pietro Giordani. Starts recording his observations in the *Zibaldone*. Falls in love for the first time: an infatuation for a distant cousin, Gertrude Cassi-Lazzari, who was visiting with her husband. Records the event in detail and writes "Il primo amore." Translates Hesiod (*Titanomachia*) and studies Dionigi d'Alicarnasso.

1818. Writes *Discorso di un italiano intorno alla poesia romantica*. Receives a visit from Pietro Giordani in September. Writes "All'Italia" and "Sopra il monumento di Dante che si preparava in Firenze," both of which will be published in Rome early the following year.

1819. Experiences the first symptoms of the eye malady that will plague him off and on for the rest of his life. Writes "L'infinito" and "Alla luna." Plans an escape from his father's house, which fails. Undergoes, at this point, a "philosophic conversion" from his childhood faith to a materialistic view of life, rooted in the rationalism and sensism of the eighteenth century and translated into an extreme form of pessimism.

1820. Records his observations on Mai's Eusebio. Writes "Ad Angelo Mai quand'ebbe trovato i libri di Cicerone della Repubblica," published in Bologna early in July. Writes "Sera del dì di festa."

1821. Writes "Nelle nozze della sorella Paolina," "A un vincitore nel pallone," "Bruto minore," and, it seems, "Il sogno" and "La vita solitaria."

1822. Writes "Alla primavera," "Ultimo canto di Saffo," and "Inno ai Patriarchi, o de' principii del genere umano." Leaves for Rome in November, to visit with his uncle, Carlo Antici. While there, completes the pseudo fourth-century account of *Martirio de' santi Padri*.

1823. While in Rome, he intensifies his philological studies and publishes his notes on new texts of Filone, on Cicero's *De re publica* and Eusebio's *Cronaca*. Returns to Recanati in May, where in September he writes "Alla sua donna."

1824. Writes the first twenty *Operette Morali* and *Discorso sopra lo stato presente dei costumi degl'italiani*. Publishes in

Bologna *Canzoni* with philological "Annotazioni."

1824-1825. Translates Isocrates, Epitectus and others of that period.

1825. In July, visits Bologna and Milan. In Milan he is the guest of the publisher Antonio Fortunato Stella.

1825-1826. The first *Idilli* appears in December 1825 and January 1826 in the *Nuovo Ricoglitore* of Milan. Meanwhile, he prepares, through the publisher Stella, an edition of Cicero's works and writes the commentary on Petrarch's *Canzoniere*. In Bologna, from October 1825 to November 1826, he enjoys the warm hospitality of Giordani and his friend Pietro Brighenti. While in Bologna, he writes the verse epistle "Al Conte Carlo Pepoli," which he reads on Easter Monday, 1826, in the Casino of the Accademia del Felsinesi. A new passion, this time for the Countess Teresa Carniani Malvezzi, an educated Bolognese noblewoman, is quickly discouraged. Also in 1826, in Bologna, he publishes *Versi*, a slim volume of poetry.

1826-1827. Assembles *Crestomazia italiana*, two anthologies of prose and poetry, respectively. During his stay in Bologna from April to June 1827, he meets Antonio Ranieri for the first time.

1827. Writes *Copernico* and *Plotino e Porfirio* (dialogues). In Florence from June to November, he is a frequent guest at the gatherings of Giampietro Vieusseux, where he is introduced to Manzoni and Gioberti. The first edition of *Operette morali* appears in Milan.

1827-1828. In Pisa, from November 1827 to June 1828, he writes "Il risorgimento" and "A Silvia."

1828-1829. Returns to Recanati in November 1828, where he writes, between the end of August and into September 1829, "Le ricordanze," "La quiete dopo la tempesta," "Il sabato del villaggio."

1829-1830. The poet's fragile health takes a turn for the

worse; it becomes almost impossible for him to continue working. Between October and April, he writes "Canto notturno di un pastore errante dell'Asia." Around this time, he also seems to have written "Il passero solitario." On April 29, 1830, he leaves Recanati — never to return — and goes to Florence.

1830-1831. The generous hospitality of the historian and general, Pietro Colletta, keeps Leopardi in Florence from May 1830 to April 1831, where he strengthens his ties with Antonio Ranieri and comes to know the erudite scholar, Luigi De Sinner. His unrequited love for Fanny Targioni-Tozzetti dates to this time. In the Spring and Summer of 1831, he writes "Il pensiero dominante," and seems to have begun, at this time, the *Paralipomeni della Batracomiomachia*, which he will continue to expand right up to the time of his death. The first edition of *Canti* appears in Florence in 1831.

1831. Leaves Florence for Rome on the first of October, accompanied by his faithful friend, Antonio Ranieri.

1832. In Rome and in Florence, where he returns in March, he writes *Dialogo di un venditore d'almanacchi e di un passeggero* and, very likely after his return to Florence, the last dialogue of the *Operette*, "Tristano e di un amico." Still in Florence, between the Summer and Fall of 1832, he writes "Amore e Morte" and, in all probability, "Consalvo." At this time, he stops writing in the *Zibaldone* (the last entry carries the date of December 4, 1832).

1833. In Florence, during the first months of the year, he writes "A se stesso" and a draft of "Inno ad Arimane," inspired, it seems, by his unrequited love for Fanny Targioni Tozzetti. He leaves Florence in September to join Ranieri in Naples. He seems to have begun editing his *Pensieri* at this time.

1834-1835. In the first months of 1834, he writes "Aspasia," the last of the poems inspired by his love for Fanny. The second edition of *Operette morali* appears in Florence. Between 1834 and 1835, he writes "Sopra un basso rilievo antico sepolcrale," and "Sopra il ritratto di una bella donna scolpito nel monumento sepolcrale della medesima."

1835. Writes "Palinodia al marchese Gino Capponi" and the satire *I nuovi credenti.* He begins to assemble, for the publisher Starita of Naples, his *Opere,* of which the first two volumes appear in the course of this year, one containing the *Canti,* the other the *Operette morali* up to "Parini o della gloria."

1836-1837. While a guest at villa Ferrigni, at the foot of Vesuvius in Torre del Greco, he writes "La ginestra o il fiore del deserto" and "Il tramonto della luna."

1837 (June 14). Dies in Naples, in the home of Antonio Ranieri.

TO THE MEMORY OF TWO EXTRAORDINARY MEN,

BOTH OF WHOM LIVED THE LIFE OF THOUGHT

AND TAUGHT OTHERS HOW TO APPRECIATE IT,

THOMAS G. BERGIN
and
HENRY PAOLUCCI

Many thanks to friends and colleagues who kept nudging me to finish this project, especially Frank D. Grande, D.Phil(Oxon), Chairman of the History Department at The City College (CUNY), and Maurice Edwards, Director-Producer-Actor-Man of Extraordinary Talents and for over twenty-five years the Artistic Director of the Brooklyn Philarmonic. They not only provided support and encouragement along the way but also read the manuscript and made valuable suggestions. Their enthusiasm helped me over the hurdles and was a major factor in my decision to complete these translations.

POEMS AND COMMENTARIES

EARLY EXCERPTS
FROM THE NOTEBOOKS (1820)

The following extracts from Leopardi's notebooks, all written between June and November of 1820, provide a brief sampling of the poet's early thoughts on death and on the distinction – to which he returns many times in later entries – between philosophy and poetry, reason and the imagination. His long brooding on these and other subjects make his entries in the various journals and letters not only interesting reading in and for themselves but, very often, illuminating "footnotes" to the poetic text, as well. Some of these passages – brought together from different sources – have also been translated and appear at the end of a number of poems, under the title "Commentary."

At a time when I was disgusted with life and without any hope at all, and so desirous of death above all else that I despaired because I could not die, a letter arrived from a friend.* He had always encouraged me to hope and to live, assuring me, as a man of high intelligence and great repute, that I would become great and bring glory to Italy. In his letter he told me to dwell on my misfortunes so that if God sent death I should accept it as a good, and he wished a quick death for himself and for me because of the love that he bore me. Would you believe that this letter, instead of detaching me to a greater degree from life, reawakened my affection for what I had already abandoned? And that thinking of my friend's past hopes, and of the words of solace, and of the expectations of the future which he now no longer seemed to care to see come true, even that greatness he had promised, and glancing upon my papers and studies and remembering my childhood, and the thoughts, desires and beautiful sights and occupations of my adolescence, my heart was wrung in such a way that I could no longer renounce hope, and death now frightened me? Not death itself, but as the annulment of all the past beautiful expectations. And yet, that letter said nothing that I had not told myself each day; it corresponded exactly to my beliefs. I find the following reasons account for this effect:

1. Things which seem tolerable from a distance change as they come nearer. The letter and wish put me in a peculiar state of mind, as though the world were shrinking, as though death truly were drawing nearer, and this death which had seemed very easy to bear from afar, which seemed even to be the only desirable thing, seemed most dreadful when imminent.

2. I thought of that desire for death as heroic. I was certain that nothing else remained for me, yet I took pleasure only in imagining death. I believed that my very few friends (but only those few and that one I spoke of above) would wish me to live, and would not resign themselves to my desperate state. I believed that if I should die they would be stunned and would say: "Then it is all finished? Oh, God, such hopes, such greatness, such talent without fruit! No glory, no pleasures, all is gone as if it had never been." But then the thought occurred to me that they might say: "Praise God, his suffering has ended. I am happy for him. He had nothing good to look forward to: may he rest in peace"; and this swift closing of the tomb above me, this sudden and complete acceptance of my death on the part of my dear ones, however reasonable, suffocated me with the thought of my complete annihilation. The anticipation of your death which consoles your friends beforehand is the most frightening thing you can imagine.

3. The state, not of my reason, which knew the truth, but of my imagination, was this. The necessity and the advantages of death, which were real, created in my mind the effect of an illusion that pleased my imagination, while the advantages and the hopes of life, which were illusory, lived deep in my heart as the reality. The letter

4

from my friend reversed these things. Thus life, without the imagination, is a death, and the most extreme misfortune becomes even worse, resembling hell itself, when you are deprived of that illusion which nature always allows. If irreparable harm comes to you and you communicate the painful event to a friend who entirely confirms what your reason had already seen too clearly, appearing to accept the totality and irreparability of the evil that has overtaken you, every last remaining hope is taken away and you fall into complete despair.

From these observations you should learn how to console one who is afflicted. Do not appear to be skeptical of his misery, if it is real. You would not persuade him, you would make him even more desolate by depriving him of your compassion. He knows his own trouble too well, and in hearing him out you will be agreeing with him. Yet, in the depths of his heart a drop of illusion is still left. Believe me, even the most desperate preserve some illusion through the continual benefit of nature. Take care not to dry it up, and wish instead to err in the mitigation of his misery; show less compassion than assurance for what his imagination opposes to his reason. Even if he exaggerates his calamity, know that in the depths of his heart he does just the opposite, and by depths I mean that most intimate recess, hidden even from himself. You must not assent to his words, but to his heart; and by encouraging his heart you will give a certain reality to that shadow of illusion remaining in him, just as you would give him the final mortal blow if you did not. Solitude and desert would have consoled him better than you, because he would have had the happiness and the consolation of nature. I speak of the very serious and real calamities, which reduce life to desperation, and not of the slight hurts which we exaggerate to make believable, nor of those arising out of grand illusions and passions, where man perhaps seeks despair and flees comfort.

In my poetic career my spirit has followed the

same course as that of the human spirit in general. In the beginning, my strength lay in my fantasy: my poems were full of images and I sought always to improve my imagination by reading poetry. I was also very sensitive to feelings, but I did not know how to express them in poetry. I had not yet meditated on the nature of things, and had only a glimmer of philosophy, and that in the broadest way, with the usual illusion that we allow ourselves, that life ought to make an exception in our favor. I have always been unfortunate, but at that time my misfortunes became especially intense; I despaired because they seemed to bar me (not in any rational way, but in my very active imagination) from the happiness which I believed others enjoyed. In short, my state of mind then was very like that of the ancients. But it is also true that when adversity gripped and tortured me most, I became capable of expressing certain feelings in poetry. The total change in me (and the passage from the ancient epoch to the modern, it could be said) occurred within one year; in 1819, when deprived of my sight and of the continual distraction of reading, I began to experience my unhappiness in a much more gloomy way, I began to lose hope and to reflect profoundly on the nature of things. (In this frame of mind I wrote in one year almost twice as much as I had written in a year and a half, and chiefly on subjects pertaining to human nature, in contrast to my past thinking which had been almost entirely concerned with literature.) I became a philosopher instead of a poet, and I began to *feel* the inevitable unhappiness of the world instead of merely being acquainted with it. This happened also because I suffered from a state of physical languor which separated me further from the ancients and brought me closer to the moderns. At this time my imagination had weakened greatly, and although my power of invention grew increasingly stronger, almost as though it had just begun, it turned however to matters of prose or the poetry of feeling. And as I set myself to the task of writing poetry, the images came to me with great difficulty; my fantasy had almost dried up, not only in the making of poetry, but also in the appreciation of the beauties of the natural world, which still leave me as unmoved as stone; those lines, however, brimmed over with feeling.

For this reason we can say that in the strictest sense there were never poets except among the ancients, and there are none today except among children and the young; the modern men we call poets are none other than philosophers. Indeed, I only began to feel when I lost my fantasy and became insensitive to nature, dedicating myself to reason and to truth; that is, when I became a philosopher. Good poetry is equally comprehensible to men who have imagination and feeling and to those who lack it, yet imaginative men take pleasure in poetry and unimaginative men do not, they do not even understand how others can take pleasure in it, primarily because they are neither able nor willing to be moved or inspired by the poet. And further, even if they understood the words, unimaginative men do not understand the truth, the obviousness of the sentiments; they do not acknowledge the reality of the passions, the effects, the moral phenomena which the poet describes. And for that matter, the poet's words, although they may be clear and completely understandable, do not represent to unimaginative men the same emotional truths that they represent to others; they understand the words but not the poet. One must observe that this same phenomenon occurs with philosophical writings as well, so do not marvel at the very different and often very opposite effects produced in individual readers of different classes, and hence by the different meanings which are created. Let us imagine such a work, full of truth and composed with the greatest clarity of expression. The words mean the same to men of profound and superficial thought; both comprehend equally well the literal sense of the writing: that is, both understand perfectly the author's meaning.

But yet that work is not understood equally, as people commonly believe it to be. For the superficial thinker, who does not know how to join his mind with the mind of the author, that is, one who is incapable of thinking with the same profundity as the author, understands the matter that he has read, but not seeing that these words are true, not feeling their rightness, failing to discover the field that the author has discovered, the superficial thinker does not recognize the connections and the consequences that the author recognized, and which for him and for all who are like him are incontrovertible. But these things are not truth to such men; they may see the same things but do not understand or feel the relationships and results the author reveals. They do not see the reciprocal relationships of the parts of the syllogism (since all human cognition is a syllogism); in short, they understand very well the work, but not the truth of it, that truth which is a reality fully comprehended by others. They do not possess sufficient insight to be able to question, to feel the reasonableness and the *truth* (*verità*) of internal doubt about what is taken, naturally or by convention, to be real. Among these persons are the majority of modern apologists of religion, men without spirit, without feeling, without discriminating or profound insight into the things of nature, indeed, without the *experience* of truth. These men are like those readers of poetry who are without the experience of passions, of enthusiasm, of feelings, who, even if they understand perfectly the meaning of those very profound philosophies with which they grapple, still do not understand the truth contained there and clearly and advisedly grant to be false what others know to be true, or grant to be true what others know to be false. Indeed, in order to understand the philosophers (and almost all other writers, including the poets), the reader must possess such strength of imagination and feeling, such a capacity for reflection, that he is able to enter into the mind of the writer and into his precise point of view and his situation; otherwise the writer will never be clear enough, however clear he actually is. And this must the reader do, whether or not he agrees with the author, whether or not he is persuaded by him.

It is not enough to understand a true proposition; one must also feel the truth of it. There is a feeling for truth, just as there is for passions, for sentiments, for beauty: for the true as for the beautiful. Whoever understands it but does not feel it understands what signifies truth but does not understand what truth is, because he has not experienced its meaning, that is, its influence on him.

---

*Letter dated June 18, 1820, from Pietro Giordani, a minor literary figure, with whom Leopardi began a correspondence in March of 1817. Giordani's interest in and encouragement of the young Leopardi had a profound effect on the poet.

IL PRIMO AMORE
(1817)

Tornami a mente il dì che la battaglia
d'amor sentii la prima volta, e dissi:
oimè, se quest'è amor, com'ei travaglia!
    Che gli occhi al suol tuttora intenti e fissi,
io mirava colei ch'a questo core
primiera il varco ed innocente aprissi.
    Ahi come mal mi governasti amore!
Perchè seco dovea sì dolce affetto
recar tanto desio, tanto dolore?
    e non sereno, e non intero e schietto,
anzi pien di travaglio e di lamento
al cor mi discendea tanto diletto?
    Dimmi, tenero core, or che spavento,
che angoscia era la tua fra quel pensiero
presso al qual t'era noia ogni contento?
    Quel pensier che nel dì, che lusinghiero
ti si offriva nella notte, quando
tutto queto parea nell'emisfero:
    tu inquieto, e felice e miserando,
m'affaticavi in su le piume il fianco,
ad ogni or fortemente palpitando.
    E dove io tristo ed affannato e stanco
gli occhi al sonno chiudea, come per febre
rotto e deliro il sonno venia manco.
    Oh come viva in mezzo alle tenebre
sorgea la dolce imago, e gli occhi chiusi
la contemplavan sotto alle palpebre!
    oh come soavissimi diffusi
moti per l'ossa mi serpeano, oh come
mille nell'alma instabili, confusi

FIRST LOVE

The day comes back to mind when
first I felt love's battle, and said: if this
is love, oh, he drives hard! When with
my eyes cast down, fixed always on the
ground, I saw her in my mind, the first
to whom I'd opened up my unsuspecting
heart. Ah, Love, how cruelly you ruled
over me! why did such sweet affection
have to bring with it such yearning,
so much pain? and so much joy, not calm,
not innocent, not simple, hard-driven
rather, full of anguish, reach down
into my heart? Tell me, my tender heart,
what dread, what pain did you feel
at that thought, compared to which
all other pleasant memories seemed dull?
That thought which lured you in daylight
and at night when all the world seemed
still: restless and happy and in pain, you
would wear me out, as I lay in bed,
pounding hard against my side,
hour after hour, and the minute
I'd close my eyes in sleep, sad and
breathless and exhausted, sleep
would be shattered as though by fever
and delirium. Oh, how real that sweet
image rose among the shadows, and my eyes,
shut tight, watched it underneath their lids!
oh how the tenderest emotions wound
themselves around my bones, how
thousands of confused uncertain

pensieri si volgean! qual tra le chiome
d'antica selva zefiro scorrendo,
un lungo incerto mormorar ne prome.

E mentre io taccio, e mentre io non contendo,
che dicevi, o mio cor, che si partia
quella per che penando ivi e battendo?

Il cuocer non più tosto io mi sentia
della vampa d'amor, che il venticello
che l'aleggiava, volossene via.

Senza sonno io giacea sul dì novello,
e i destrier che dovean farmi deserto,
battean la zampa sotto al patrio ostello.

Ed io timido e cheto ed inesperto,
ver lo balcone al buio protendea
l'orecchio avido e l'occhio indarno aperto,

la voce ad ascoltar, se ne dovea
di quelle labbra uscir, ch'ultima fosse;
la voce, ch'altro il cielo, ahi, mi togliea.

Quante volte plebea voce percosse
il dubitoso orecchio, e un gel mi prese,
e il core in forse a palpitar si mosse!

E poi che finalmente mi discese
la cara voce al core, e de' cavai
e delle rote il romorio s'intese;

orbo rimaso allor, mi rannichiai
palpitando nel letto e, chiusi gli occhi,
strinsi il cor con la mano, e sospirai.

Poscia traendo i tremuli ginocchi
stupidamente per la muta stanza,
ch'altro sarà, dicea, che il cor mi tocchi?

Amarissima allor la ricordanza
locommisi nel petto, e mi serrava
ad ogni voce il core, a ogni sembianza.

E lunga doglia il sen mi ricercava,

thoughts churned inside me! like the wind
rushing through the branches of a thick forest
sets up a long uncertain murmuring.
And though I said nothing and though
I offer no objection, what were you saying,
dear heart, when she was leaving, she for
whom you had been pining and beating
so hard? No sooner did I feel the flame
of love burn in me than the breeze that fed it
went away. I lay awake, sleepless at dawn,
and the horses that would turn my life into
a desert, stamped their hooves outside my
father's house. And, shy and quiet and new
at this, I turned my eager ears toward the
balcony, my eyes open in vain in the dark,
my ears straining to catch her voice,
if it were to issue from those lips one last
time, the voice, for heaven, alas, was taking
from me all the rest. How many times some
grating voice struck my uncertain ear,
and a chill gripped me, and my heart
started to pound in suspense! And when at last
that dear voice reached down into my heart,
and the clatter of horses and carriage wheels
was heard; left alone, then, bereft, I curled up
breathless in my bed and closed my eyes,
pressed my hand against my heart, and
sighed. Later, dragging my quaking knees
in aimless pacing of the quiet room, I kept
repeating, after this, what else can touch
my heart? I locked, then, inside my breast
that most bitter memory, and shut my heart
to every other voice to every face.
And a long sadness settled in my breast,

com'è quando a distesa Olimpo piove
malinconicamente e i campi lava.

Ned io ti conoscea, garzon di nove
e nove Soli, in questo a pianger nato
quando facevi, amor, le prime prove.

Quando in ispregio ogni piacer, né grato
m'era degli astri il riso, o dell'aurora
queta il silenzio, o il verdeggiar del prato.

Anche di gloria amor taceami allora
nel petto, cui scaldar tanto solea,
che di beltade amor vi fea dimora.

Né gli occhi ai noti studi io rivolgea,
e quelli m'apparian vani per cui
vano ogni altro desir creduto avea.

Deh come mai da me sì vario fui,
e tanto amor mi tolse un altro amor?
deh quanto, in verità, vani siam nui!

Solo il mio cor piaceami, e col mio core
in un perenne ragionar sepolto,
alla guardia seder del mio dolore.

E l'occhio a terra chino o in sé raccolto,
di riscontrarsi fuggitivo e vago
né in leggiadro soffria né in turpe volto:

che la illibata, la candida imago
turbare egli temea pinta nel seno,
come all'aure si turba onda di lago.

E quel di non aver goduto appieno
pentimento, che l'anima ci grava,
e il piacer che passò cangia in veleno,

per li fuggiti dì mi stimolava
tuttora il sen: che la vergogna il duro
suo morso in questo cor già non oprava.

Al cielo, a voi, gentili anime, io giuro
che voglia non m'entrò bassa nel petto,

as when Olympus rains sorrowfully,
ceaselessly, and washes down the fields.
Nor did I know you, love, when first
you put me to the test, a boy twice nine
suns old, destined to tears in this present one.
When every pleasure was held in scorn, nor was
I grateful for the stars' smile, or the silence
of the peaceful dawn, or the meadow turning
green. Even love of fame, that used to warm
my breast, was silent now; for love of beauty
had settled there. Nor did I turn my eyes
to familiar studies, and those seemed useless
compared to which I had deemed useless,
earlier, all other things.
Ah, how could I from myself have changed
so much, and another love take from me
so much love? Ah, truth is, how empty we all are!
Only my heart was pleasing to me, and to be
buried in endless reasoning with my heart,
to stand guard over my pain.
And my eyes lowered to the ground or
turned within, fleeting and uncertain,
avoided looking into faces, fair or ugly,
lest they disturb the chaste pure image
painted in my heart, like dawn disturbs
the waters of a lake.
And that regret at not having lived life
fully, which weighs heavy on the soul
and turns old pleasures to poison,
now made me yearn for days
gone by: for shame had not then left
its bitter sting inside my heart. I swear
to heaven, to all you gentle souls,
that no base desire moved my heart,

15

ch'arsi di fuoco intaminato e puro.
   Vive quel foco ancor, vive l'affetto,
spira nel pensier mio la bella imago,
da cui, se non celeste, altro diletto
   giammai non ebbi, e sol di lei m'appago.

that I burned with pure chaste fire.
It still lives, that fire, that tenderness,
in my thoughts the lovely image
still breathes from which I never drew
anything but celestial joy,
and in it alone I rest content.

COMMENTARY

For over a year, after I began to feel the full power of beauty, I craved to meet and talk with attractive women (as we all do) . . . . And in my rigorous self-inflicted solitude, this desire remained an empty one until recently. Then on the evening of Thursday last [December 11, 1817], a woman from Pesaro [Gertrude Cassi], whom I had never met before but whose arrival I looked forward to with tremendous pleasure, as my long-awaited chance to satisfy the desire for such an exchange, came to visit us. She was a distance relative, about twenty-six years old, and came with her husband [Giov. Giuseppe Lazzari], who was over fifty — a large and placid man. She herself was tall and big-boned, more so than any other woman I have ever seen; but her face was by no means ordinary or gross. Her features were strong yet delicate; her entire color, fine; her eyes, very black; her hair, a chestnut shade; her manner, pleasant and I thought graceful, without a trace of affectation and far from ordinary — typical of the women of the Romagna and particularly those of Pesaro, so very different (in a way that escapes definition) from our women here in the Marche.

I was not disappointed that evening, when I first saw her; but I spoke to her only briefly and made no great effort. On Friday, I talked to her rather abruptly just before lunch. We ate together — I, in my usual quiet mood but observing her all the while with a cold and curious longing to study such an attractive face, a longing more intense than any contemplation of a beautiful painting . . . . Friday evening, my brothers played cards with her . . . and as I watched her, I wanted desperately to play cards with her myself, so as to

17

satisfy that craving in me to talk with an attractive woman . . . .
The next day I waited for the card game with pleasure, but
without excitement or anxious anticipation . . . . Finally, I did
join her at cards. I came out of it frustrated and deeply
troubled . . . . The woman had treated me graciously, and for
the first time I had succeeded in making an attractive lady
laugh at my jokes and stories; I had talked with her and she
had answered and smiled. I tried to explain to myself the
reason for my dissatisfaction but could not grasp it . . . . It
seemed to me that I had succeeded in obtaining what I had
wanted — all that I could possibly have anticipated and that
the fault was neither here nor there. Still, my feelings were
very tender and pleasant as I took in the woman's gestures
and words at dinner. I was drawn to her and liked her even
more . . . . Later, alone in my room, I examined my feelings,
which were — I had to admit — indefinable and restless, full of
sadness, dissatisfaction, for I know not what . . . . I lingered
over the lively and vivid memories of that evening and of the
preceding day, and thus lay awake for hours, until finally I fell
asleep and dreamt — in a kind of fever — of cards, games, the
woman herself . . . all those motions which had taken hold of
me and had inserted themselves in my thoughts and which
would not let go of me, even in sleep. I woke up at daybreak
and did not fall asleep again. Instead, I began to go over
everything that had happened (understandable, under the
circumstances), or, rather, continued those reflections from
before . . . . The window of my room overlooks a courtyard . .
. . and when I heard people moving about below, I realized
that our guests were getting ready to leave. I listened both
patiently and impatiently as the horses were brought around,
and then the carriage; people coming and going, my ears
straining all the while for the moment the woman would
appear, anxious to hear her voice one last time . . . and at last
I heard it.

A bitter pang strikes me each time I recall those days,
memories sadder than I could ever describe; and when certain
hours and circumstances come around, I am reminded of
those events and can't help thinking again of the great

18

emptiness that weighted so heavily on me.

If this is love — something new to me — it is the first time that I have experienced it as an adult and can examine it. Here I am, nineteen and a half years old, in love. And I can see all too clearly that falling in love is a most bitter thing, and that, unfortunately, I shall always be vulnerable with respect to tender and sentimental attachments.

I can never be ashamed of my passion; in fact, from the very first moment I experienced it, I have found tremendous satisfaction in it, pleased that I can respond to those feelings without which a person cannot find greatness, and happy in the knowledge that I can be moved by other things than the satisfactions of the body and that experience has convinced me that I have a tender and sensitive nature, which some day may enable me to do or write something that will live in the memory or that will bring me some satisfaction, . . . I don't deny, therefore, that I have cultivated and encouraged such emotions in recent times; and that the let-down I felt when I realized those feelings were dissipating was in part due to my inclination and desire to experience everything, including love. I have always despised any suggestion of sentimentality, . . . nor do I find pleasure in reading love stories for . . . the emotions of others — even when described with sincerity — turn my stomach. I can't even take Petrarch, who — I thought — would surely describe feelings very like mine.

(Scritti vari, 1817)

L'INFINITO
(1819)

Sempre caro mi fu quest'ermo colle,
e questa siepe che da tanta parte
dell'ultimo orizzonte il guardo esclude.
Ma sedendo e mirando, interminati
spazi di là da quella, e sovrumani
silenzi, e profondissima quiete
io nel pensier mi fingo; over per poco
il cor non si spaura. E come il vento
odo stormir tra queste piante, io quello
infinito silenzio a questa voce
vo comparando: e mi sovvien l'eterno,
e le morte stagioni, e la presente
e viva, e il suon di lei. Così tra questa
immensità s'annega il pensier mio:
e il naufragar m'è dolce in questo mare.

THE INFINITE

This lonely hill was always dear to me,
and this hedge, which cuts off from view
the far horizon on almost every side.
But sitting here and gazing about me,
my mind conceives limitless stretches
beyond it, silences more than human,
and the profoundest calm; so that the heart
almost shrinks in fear. And as I listen
to the wind rustle through these branches,
I find myself comparing that infinite silence
to this voice, and the eternal comes to mind,
and the dead seasons and the present living
one, and the sound of it. Then in the midst
of this immensity my thought drowns:
and sinking is sweet to me in such a sea.

COMMENTARY

As for those sensations that please precisely because
they are indefinite (see my poem on the Infinite): picture a
stretch of countryside declining so steeply that from a certain
distance the eye cannot reach the valley, a line of trees which
cannot be traced to the very end either because the line itself
stretches too far or because it too descends steeply, etc. A
building, a tower on the horizon, seen in such a way as to
appear suspended there, produce a powerful and awesome
contrast between finite and infinite.

(Pensieri III, 8/1/1821)

That portion of my theory of pleasure in which
objects half-seen or seen through obstacles are shown to
arouse vague and indefinite thoughts explains why it is that
the light of the sun or moon is pleasing when seen where
these themselves cannot be seen and the source of light

remains hidden; why an area only partly illuminated by such light is pleasing, or the reflection of such light and the physical effects it produces; or the filtering of such light into places where it becomes hazy and meets obstacles and cannot be discerned clearly, as across a cane field, or in a forest, through half-closed balconies, etc.; or the same light seen in a place where it does not enter or hit anything directly but is cast there by reflection and diffusion from some other place or object which it does hit; a gallery, from inside or outside, an enclosed porch, etc.; those places where light and shadows are indistinguishable, as under a portico, in an elevated over-hanging balcony, among cliffs and ravines, in a valley, on hills bathed in light; the reflection produced by tinted glass, for instance, on objects which are seen through various sub-stances and under such conditions, or which are heard indistinctly, in a confused imperfect incomplete or unusual way. On the other hand, the sight of the sun or moon in vast sprawling country and in an open sky is pleasing because of the sensation of vastness. And also pleasing, for the reason mentioned earlier, is the sight of a sky scattered unevenly with tiny clouds, where the light of the sun or moon produces various indistinct and unusual effects. The same light is most pleasing and romantic as seen in the city where it is slashed by shadows, where the dark in many places vies with the luminous; where light diminishes little by little, as on roofs, where some hidden places obstruct the view of the shining orb, etc. This pleasing sensation is enhanced by variety and uncertainty, by not seeing everything and therefore being able, with the imagination, to sweep over and encompass what is actually not seen.

(Pensieri III, 9/20/1821)

What I have said in connection with the infinite, about the effects produced by light or visible objects, must be ex-tended to include sound and singing, as well — all that be-longs to the auditory. Singing (no matter how poor) heard from afar, or that seems far off, though it is not, or that gradually recedes and grows imperceptible — or the opposite (though less striking) — is pleasing in and for itself, that is, for no other reason except the vague and indefinite sensation it arouses; or singing that seems or actually is so far off that ear and thought almost lose it in the vastness of distance; or an ordinary somewhat confused sound, especially if it is so because of distance; singing heard without our being able to see where it comes from; singing that echoes in the vaults of a hall in which, however, you are not present; the singing of farmhands, ringing across the countryside and over the valleys without our actually seeing them; the lowing of herds, etc. Hearing sounds or singing from the street, while indoors, especially late at night, one is more susceptible to these effects because neither hearing nor the other senses can then determine or circumscribe sensation and all its manifestations . . . . To these observations we must add the pleasure which can be and is produced — when not overwhelmed by fear — by the crash of thunder, especially when it is almost wholly muffled, when heard in open country; the rush of the wind, especially in those circumstances where it moves confusedly in a forest or among the various objects of the countryside . . . . These images are always exceedingly beautiful in poetry, and all the more so when inserted casually, and touching on these matters without any explanation.

(Pensieri III, 10/16/1821)

ALLA LUNA
(1819)

O graziosa luna, io mi rammento
che, or volge l'anno, sovra questo colle
io venia pien d'angoscia a rimirarti:
e tu pendevi allor su quella selva
siccome or fai, che tutta la rischiari.
Ma nebuloso e tremulo dal pianto
che mi sorgea sul ciglio, alle mie luci
il tuo volto apparia, che travagliosa
era mia vita: ed è, né cangia stile,
o mia diletta luna. E pur mi giova
la ricordanza, e il noverar l'etate
del mio dolore. Oh come grato occorre
nel tempo giovanil, quando ancor lungo
la speme e breve ha la memoria il corso,
il rimembrar delle passate cose,
ancor che triste, e che l'affanno duri!

TO THE MOON

Oh gracious moon, I remember coming
to this hill almost a year ago,
full of grief, to gaze at you: and you
were poised then above those woods
as you are now, lighting them all up.
But to my eyes your face seemed hazy
and wavering through the tears
that rose in me, for my life was oppressive:
and still is, nor will it change in any way,
my darling moon. And yet I find relief
remembering and counting the time
of my pain. Oh, how comforting
to call up things in the past, though sad,
and though the suffering persists,
the early years, when hope still has a way
to go, and memory, a short run only.

COMMENTARY

For some time now I have been unable to see or think
on account of a weakening of the optical nerves that makes it
impossible for me not only to read or study but also to
exercise my mind in any way. You can well imagine, I'm sure,
the kind of life I have been leading, stripped as I am of the
only comfort available to me in this kind of place and in my
circumstances.

(Letter to Count Trissino, September 27, 1819)

I am so completely overwhelmed by the sheer
nothingness that surrounds us that I can hardly pick up my
pen to answer your letter of the 1st. If I were to go mad at this
very moment, I think that madness would take the form of my
sitting forever like this, staring in front of me, my mouth
open, my hands between my knees, never laughing, weeping,

or moving from my seat without a great effort. I have no strength left even to wish for anything, not even death; not because I fear it in any way, but because I don't see the slightest differences between death and the life I lead, in which even the relief of pain has been denied me. This is the first time that such emptiness not only overwhelms and tires me but also weighs on me like an unbearable affliction; and I am terrified, now that all emotion has died in me, that I am quite beside myself, knowing that even my despair is an empty thing.

(Letter to Giordani, November 19, 1819)

The richest and most lively of our memories are those delightful and poetic images that have to do with childhood and all that it suggests (words, phrases, poems, paintings, real or imitated) . . . . And especially pleasing because of their realistic impact are memories or images of things that in our youth seemed frightening and painful. In the same way, throughout life, we find a certain pleasure even in painful memories, even when the reason for the pain is still an immediate reality, as the death of dear ones, memories of the past, etc.

(Pensieri III, October 25, 1821)

Nor should we feel oppressed as we review painful events in the past, because the memory of things past is dear to us — not only as intimate sorrows that have left their mark, but even as they happened.

(Scritti vari, 1829)

26

THE HILLS AROUND RECANATI

THE "BORGO" TOWER

LA SERA DEL DÌ DI FESTA
(1820)

Dolce e chiara è la notte e senza vento,
e queta sovra i tetti e in mezzo agli orti
posa la luna, e di lontan rivela
serena ogni montagna. O donna mia,
già tace ogni sentiero, e pei balconi
rara traluce la notturna lampa:
tu dormi, che t'accolse agevol sonno
nelle tue chete stanze; e non ti morde
cura nessuna; e già non sai né pensi
quanta piaga m'apristi in mezzo al petto.
Tu dormi: in questo ciel, che sì benigno
appare in vista, a salutar m'affaccio,
e l'antica natura onnipotente,
che mi fece all'affanno. A te la speme
nego, mi disse, anche la speme; e d'altro
non brillin gli occhi tuoi se non di pianto.
Questo dì fu solenne; or da' trastulli
prendi riposo; e forse ti rimembra
in sogno a quanti oggi piacesti, e quanti
piacquero a te: non io, non già, ch'io speri
al pensier ti ricorro. Intanto io cheggio
quanto a viver mi resti, e qui per terra
mi getto, e grido, e fremo. Oh giorni orrendi
in così verde etate! Ahi, per la via
odo non lunge il solitario canto
dell'artigian, che riede a tarda notte,
dopo i sollazzi, al suo povero ostello;
e fieramente mi si stringe il core,
a pensar come tutto al mondo passa,
e quasi orma non lascia. Ecco è fuggito

EVENING, AFTER
THE HOLIDAY

Sweet and clear is the night, and without wind,
and the moon rests quiet over rooftops and
among orchards, and reveals every mountain
peaceful in the distance. Oh, my own dear
love, the paths are silent now and night lights
rarely flicker on the balconies: you sleep,
for slumber welcomed you in your quiet rooms;
and not a single worry gnaws at you; and you
can't possibly know or imagine how deep a
wound you opened in my breast. You sleep:
I lean out to greet this sky, that seems so
pleasant to our sight, and age-old omnipotent
nature that shaped me for suffering. To you
I deny hope, she said, even hope; and your
eyes will not shine except with tears. This was
a special day; you rest now from all the
excitement; and, in sleep you may remember
how many found you pleasing this day,
and how many you found pleasing: not I,
I surely would never dream you'd think of me.
Instead I ask how much longer I must live,
and throw myself to the ground, and shout
and tremble. Oh, dreadful days at such an
early age! Ah, a short distance down the road
I hear the solitary singing of the fieldhand,
who comes back to his poor dwelling late
at night, after the day's pleasures; and the
thought of how all passes from this world
and leaves almost no trace behind pierces
my heart. See how the holiday has fled

il dì festivo, ed al festivo il giorno
volgar succede, e se ne porta il tempo
ogni umano accidente. Or dov'è il suono
di que' popoli antichi? or dov'è il grido
de' nostri avi famosi, e il grande impero
di quella Roma, e l'armi, e il fragorio
che n'andò per la terra e l'oceano?
Tutto è pace e silenzio, e tutto posa
il mondo, e più di lor non si ragiona.
Nella mia prima età, quando s'aspetta
bramosamente il dì festivo, or poscia
ch'egli era spento, io doloroso, in veglia,
premea le piume; ed alla tarda notte
un canto che s'udia per li sentieri
lontanando morire a poco a poco,
già similmente mi stringeva il core.

and after the holiday the work day follows,
and time sweeps away every human happening.
Where now is the sound of those ancient
peoples? where now is the fame of our
renowned precursors, and the great empire
that once was Rome, its armies, and all
the stir they caused on land and sea? All is
peace and silence, and the whole world
rests, and nothing more is said of them.
In my young age, when the holiday is
eagerly anticipated, I would lie awake in bed
when it was over, full of sadness; and late
into the night, singing heard moving away
down the lanes, to die out, little by little, would
squeeze my heart in the same way, then.

BRUTO MINORE
(1821)

Poi che divelta, nella tracia polve
giacque ruina immensa
l'italica virtute, onde alle valli
d'Esperia verde, e al tiberino lido,
il calpestio de' barbari cavalli
prepara il fato, e dalle selve ignude
cui l'Orsa algida preme,
a spezzar le romane inclite mura
chiama i gotici brandi;
sudato, e molle di fraterno sangue,
Bruto per l'atra notte in erma sede,
fermo già di morir, gl'inesorandi
numi e l'averno accusa,
e di feroci note
invan la sonnolenta aura percote.

Stolta virtù, le cave nebbie, i campi
dell'inquiete larve
son le tue scole, e ti si volge a tergo
il pentimento. A voi, marmorei numi
(se numi avete in Flegetonte albergo
o su le nubi), a voi ludibrio e scherno
è la prole infelice
a cui templi chiedeste, e frodolenta
legge al mortale insulta.
Dunque tanto i celesti odii commove
la terrena pietà? dunque degli empi
siedi, Giove, a tutela? e quando esulta
per l'aere il nembo, e quando
il tuon rapido spingi,

BRUTUS THE YOUNGER

Once uprooted, Italy's awesome
strength lay, a massive ruin, in the
Thracian dust; from which fate readies
the green Hesperian valleys and the
Tiber's banks for hoofbeats of barbarian
horses, and from the bare forests
under the icy Bear, calls in Gothic swords
to hack down proud Roman walls;
all sweat and dripping with his kindred's
blood, Brutus sits alone through
the deep night; determined now to die,
he charges the inexorable gods of heaven
and hell, and pierces the sleepy
air in vain with his fierce cries.

"Foolish virtue, empty clouds,
fields of troubled fantasies
are your schools, and repentance
is offered to your back. For you,
gods of marble (if you have gods
in Phlegethon or in the clouds), for you,
mere sport and mockery this
unhappy race, from whom
you ordered temples once,
and with deceitful laws insult us mortals.
So, then, does earthly piety stir up
so much celestial hatred? so, then,
do you sit there, Jove, to protect
the wicked? and when clouds churn up
the atmosphere, and when you follow,
swift, with thunder, is it against the pious

ne' giusti e pii la sacra fiamma stringi?

Preme il destino invitto e la ferrata
necessità gl'infermi
schiavi di morte: e se a cessar non vale
gli oltraggi lor, de' necessarii danni
si consola il plebeo. Men duro è il male
che riparo non ha? dolor non sente
chi di speranza è nudo?
Guerra mortale, eterna, o fato indegno,
teco il prode guerreggia,
di cedere inesperto; e la tiranna
tua destra, allor che vincitrice il grava,
indomito scrollando si pompeggia,
quando nell'alto lato
l'amaro ferro intride,
e maligno alle nere ombre sorride.

Spiace agli Dei chi violento irrompe
nel Tartato. Non fôra
tanto valor ne' molli eterni petti.
Forse i travagli nostri, e forse il cielo
i casi acerbi e gl'infelici affetti
giocondo agli ozi suoi spettacol pose?
Non fra sciagure e colpe,
ma libera ne' boschi e pura etade
natura a noi prescrisse,
Reina un tempo e Diva. Or poi ch'a terra
sparse i regni beati empio costume,
e viver macro ad altre leggi addisse;
quando gl'infausti giorni
virile alma ricusa,
riede natura, e il non suo dardo accusa?

and the just, that sacred fire?

"Unvanquished destiny and implacable
necessity oppress the sickly slaves
of death; and if there is no way to put
an end to the abuse, the common man
resigns himself to necessary ills.
Is injury without remedy less hard
to bear? Does someone stripped of hope
not suffer grief? The brave man,
not given to surrender, wages never-ending
war against you, unworthy fate;
and when your despotic hand
in triumph weighs down heavy on him,
undaunted, he shakes it off, assuming
a proud bearing as he thrusts deep
into his side the bitter blade, and smiles
sardonic into the dark shadows.

"Unwelcome to the gods is one who,
violent, breaks into Tartarus. Such
courage is not found in weak eternal
breasts. Maybe heaven staged our labors,
and maybe our bitter trials and unhappy
feelings as pleasant show for its idle hours?
Nature, our Queen and Goddess both,
did not prescribe grief and guilt for us
but an existence free and innocent
in the woods. Now, since evil custom
has destroyed the blessed reigns
on earth and forced on it a petty life
and different laws; when a strong soul
refutes a life of misery, does nature
laugh and blame a weapon not her own?

Di colpa ignare e de' lor proprii danni
le fortunate belve
serena adduce al non previsto passo
la tarda età. Ma se spezzar la fronte
ne' rudi tronchi, o da montano sasso
dare al vento precipiti le membra,
lor suadesse affanno;
al misero desio nulla contesa
legge arcana farebbe
o tenebroso ingegno. A voi, fra quante
stirpi il cielo avvivò, soli fra tutte,
figli di Prometeo, la vita increbbe;
a voi le morte ripe,
se il fato ignavo pende,
soli, o miseri, a voi Giove contende.

E tu dal mar cui nostro sangue irriga,
candida luna, sorgi,
e l'inquieta notte e la funesta
all'ausonio valor campagna esplori.
Cognati petti il vincitor calpesta,
fremono i poggi, dalle somme vette
Roma antica ruina;
tu sì placida sei? Tu la nascente
lavinia prole, e gli anni
lieti vedesti, e i memorandi allori;
e tu su l'alpe l'immutato raggio
tacita verserai quando ne' danni
del servo italo nome,
sotto barbaro piede
rintronerà quella solinga sede.

Ecco tra nudi sassi o in verde rame
e la fera e l'augello,

"Insensible of guilt or of their plight,
beasts have the good fortune to be led
by serene advancing age to an
unsuspected end. But if cracking their skulls
against the sturdy trunks of trees or flinging
themselves into space from craggy
mountain tops, eases their pain,
their miserable whim would not be
questioned by mysterious laws or
cryptic reasoning. To you alone, children
of Prometheus, you only, of all the many
species fashioned by heaven,
life proved oppressive; to you alone,
poor wretches, only to you
does Jove deny the shores of death,
when sluggish fate delays.

    "And you, pale moon, rise from the sea
that flows with our blood, to explore
this uneasy night and the countryside
where Ausonia's strength was spent.
The victor tramples kinsmen's breasts,
the hills shudder, from her lofty
heights great Rome collapses; and you,
so peaceful? You saw Lavinia's race begin,
and happy years, and crowns of victory;
and you will cast your silent
unchanging rays over the alps,
when in the wake of servile Italy's
shame, that abandoned place
will echo under barbarian feet.

    "See, here among the stones
and on green branches, bird and beast,

del consueto obblio gravido il petto,
l'alta ruina ignora e le mutate
sorti del mondo: e come prima il tetto
rosseggerà del villanello industre,
al mattutino canto
quel desterà le valli, e per le balze
quella l'inferma plebe
agiterà delle minore belve.
Oh casi! oh gener vano! abbietta parte
siam delle cose; e non le tinte glebe,
non gli ululati spechi
turbò nostra sciagura,
nè scolorò le stelle umana cura.

    Non io d'Olimpo e di Cocito i sordi
regi, o la terra indegna,
e non la notte moribondo appello;
non te, dell'atra morte ultimo raggio,
conscia futura età. Sdegnoso avello
placâr singulti, ornâr parole e doni
di vil caterva? In peggio
precipitano i tempi; e mal s'affida
a putridi nepoti
l'onor d'egregie menti e la suprema
de' miseri vendetta. A me dintorno
le penne il bruno augello avido roti;
prema la fera, e il nembo
tratti l'ignota spoglia;
e l'aura il nome e la memoria accoglia.

their breast heavy with familiar sleep,
ignore the colossal ruin and the changed
destiny of the world: and no sooner
does the first glow of morning redden
the top of the industrious fieldhand's hut
than the one will wake with his song
the whole valley, the other will threaten
the weak among the crowd of lesser
beasts on the slopes. Oh, chance events!
oh, vain generation! We are the least part
of things; and neither bloody clods
nor caves echoing with our cries have
any impact on our calamity; nor did
our troubles pale the stars.

"Dying here, I do not call upon the deaf
gods of Olympus or Cocytus, and a world
unworthy, or the night; nor on you,
enlightened age to come, the last glimmer
before black death. A haughty soul appeased
by sobs from the wretched mob? honored
by their words and gifts? Our times rush
toward much worse; and to entrust the honor
of great minds, the ultimate revenge
of the oppressed, to putrid followers,
is poor judgment. Let the dark bird flap
his wings in eagerness around me;
let the beast attack me, and let the clouds
scatter my unmarked remains and sweep up
my name my memory and my fame."

COMMENTARY

How many times I have been driven — in spite of
myself — to curse with the dying Brutus this kind of virtue. It's

39

unfortunate that the phrase should have cast doubt upon his own virtue, especially when (experience has convinced me) it is the most eloquent proof he could have given of that virtue in himself, and an excellent reason for us to praise him.

(Epistolario I. To Pietro Giordani, 4/26/1819)

I've always been torn by the notion of virtue. My plan [to leave his father's house] was not a crime; but I am perfectly capable of sin. They were shocked when I said that to me virtue has always seemed useless. The force and immediacy of my emotions may certainly result in good; but if those same emotions were to lead me to evil, they would not be disappointed . . . . I am always stunned in discovering that those who have loved virtue from the time they were born should give themselves recklessly to sin.

(Epistolario I. 8/13/1819)

When a man is truly unfortunate, he recognizes and feels deeply the impossibility of happiness and the overwhelming certainty of human sorrow, and he grows indifferent to everything around him . . . . But if misfortune becomes unbearable, indifference is no longer enough . . . . He begins to despise life, human existence generally and himself; he becomes his own worst enemy; and at that moment, the prospect of new misfortunes and the possibility of suicide provoke in him a terrible and almost inhuman manic mood . . . . At that moment, he will give way to a bitter, evil, and ironic smile, like that of a cruel man who has succeeded — after an inflexible, prolonged, and gnawing desire — in avenging himself, a smile that is the ultimate expression of extreme despair and insupportable suffering.

(Pensieri I. 1819)

We're always appealing to future generations . . . . But I'm not clear as to what is to be gained by such an appeal. We might be better off appealing to the past; the fact is, the world grows worse and worse as it goes on . . . . The best generations are not those before us but those behind us; and it's hardly likely that the world will change and go back instead of forward. And going forward obviously it can only get worse.

(Pensieri I. 11/10/1820)

We are all thoroughly alienated from nature and therefore most unhappy. We hope for death continuously and most ardently as the only obvious and calculated remedy for our misery . . . . But what can possibly match the misery of knowing that obstacles stand in the way of death — the obstacles of religion or of the inexorable, overwhelming, inevitable, and unremitting uncertainly of our beginnings, our destiny, our end, and what awaits us after death. I realize that nature rejects suicide with everything in her power, and that suicide — more than any other human failing — undermines all her laws in the most serious way. But since nature has altogether changed us, since our lives have ceased to be "natural," . . . since that desire for death (which, according to nature, we should never even have framed) has in fact taken hold in us through the force of reason and in spite of nature, why should that same reason keep us from realizing it and thus correct in the only way possible the ills that she alone is responsible for? Why, when reason has succeeded in overwhelming and defeating nature for having made us so miserable, does it join forces with her, pushing our misery to an unbearable point and making it impossible for us to put an end to it ourselves?

(Pensieri II. 3/19/1821)

The truth is, in no other living thing do we find this desire to put an end to life; . . . nor do we find in other animals the courage to put an end to it spontaneously. But even if there were in the nature of beasts the possibility for such decisions, there would be for them no obstacle in the way of death — no commandment, no doubt would sway them from putting an end to their suffering. But even in this, you make us less than the beasts . . . . So that, the only living being who is capable of wishing for death — he alone finds it impossible to die by his own hand.

(Operette morali, Dialogo di Plotino e di Porfirio)

ULTIMO CANTO DI SAFFO
(1822)

Placida notte, e verecondo raggio
della cadente luna; e tu che spunti
fra la tacita selva in su la rupe,
nunzio del giorno; oh dilettose e care
mentre ignote mi fûr l'erinni e il fato,
sembianze agli occhi miei; già non arride
spettacol molle ai disperati affetti.
Noi l'insueto allor gaudio ravviva
quando per l'etra liquido si volve
e per li campi trepidanti il flutto
polveroso de' Noti, e quando il carro,
grave carro di Giove a noi sul capo,
tonando, il tenebroso aere divide.
Noi per le balze e le profonde valli
natar giova tra' nembi, e noi la vasta
fuga de' greggi sbiggottiti, o d'alto
fiume alla dubbia sponda
il suono e la vittrice ira dell'onda.

Bello il tuo manto, o divo cielo, e bella
sei tu, rorida terra. Ahi di cotesta
infinita beltà parte nessuna
alla misera Saffo i numi e l'empia
sorte non fenno. A' tuoi superbi regni
vile, o natura, e grave ospite addetta,
e dispregiata amante, alle vezzoze
tue forme il core e le pupille invano
supplichevole intendo. A me non ride
l'aprico margo, e dall'eterea porta
il mattutino albor; me non il canto
dei colorati augelli, e non de' faggi
il murmure saluta: e dove all'ombra

SAPPHO'S LAST SONG

Oh, tranquil night, and modest ray
of the setting moon; and you that rise
among the silent woods above the cliff,
day's harbinger; oh, dear and lovely sights
to my eyes, while fate and the furies
were unknown to me; now, sweet scenes
no longer smile on my despairing moods.
That old pleasure, now rare, animates us
again, when dusty winds from the North
sweep through the sodden air and over
trembling fields, and when the chariot,
Jove's heavy chariot, thundering over
our heads, rends the murky atmosphere.
We rejoice swimming through clouds
along ridges, and into deep valleys,
and in the scattered flight of frightened
herds, or in the sound and conquering
fury of waters from the swollen river
on the threatened shore.

Beautiful your mantle, oh sky divine,
and beautiful, you dewy earth. Alas, no part
of all this infinite beauty did the gods
and cruel fate design for unhappy Sappho.
Destined to be a wretched and oppressive
guest, a scorned lover in your superb
realms, oh nature, I turn my heart and
eyes in vain entreaty toward your
pretty sights. The sunny shores,
the early dawn emerging from the
eastern gate, do not smile for me;
the song of brightly colored birds
and the murmur of beeches hold no
greeting for me, and where in the shadow

43

degli'inchinati salici dispiega
candido rivo il puro seno, al mio
lubrico piè le flessuose linfe
disdegnando sottrage,
e preme in fuga l'odorate spiagge.

Qual fallo mai, qual sì nefando eccesso
macchiommi anzi il natale, onde sì torvo
il ciel mi fosse e di fortuna il volto?
In che peccai bambina, allor che ignara
di misfatto è la vita, onde poi scemo
di giovanezza, e disfiorato, al fuso
dell'indomita Parca si volvesse
il ferrigno mio stame? Incaute voci
spande il tuo labbro: i destinati eventi
move arcano consiglio. Arcano è tutto,
fuor che il nostro dolor. Negletta prole
nascemmo al pianto, e la ragione in grembo
de' celesti si posa. Oh, cure, oh speme
de' più verd'anni! Alle sembianze il Padre,
alle amene sembianze eterno regno
diè nelle genti; e per virili imprese,
per dotta lira o canto,
virtù non luce in disadorno ammanto.

Morremmo. Il velo indegno a terra sparto,
rifuggirà l'ignudo animo a Dite,
e il crudo fallo emenderà del cieco
dispensator de' casi. E tu cui lungo
amore indarno, e lunga fede, e vano
d'implacato desio furor mi strinse,
vivi felice, se felice in terra
visse nato mortal. Me non asperse
del soave licor del doglio avaro
Giove, poi che perîr gl'inganni e il sogno
della mia fanciullezza. Ogni più lieto
giorno di nostra età primo s'invola.

44

of bending willows the clear stream bares
its pure breast, the nimble waters
scornfully elude my slippery step and,
in flight, press down the fragrant banks.

What fault was mine, what horrible
excess marked me before birth, that heaven
and fortune should turn so cruel a face
toward me? How did I sin, a child, when life
knows no evil, that later, the hard thread
of my life should turn on the spindle of
implacable Fate, deprived and deflowered
of its youth? Your lips spread careless words:
obscure decrees move destined events.
Everything is obscure, except our suffering.
Neglected children, we were born to tears,
and the reason rests in the bosom of the gods.
Oh cares and hopes of our most tender years!
Our Father gave to appearances,
to pleasing appearances, eternal sway
over mankind; and for worthy deeds,
for skilled playing or singing, virtue
does not shine in plain ordinary dress.

We shall die. Once this unworthy veil
is shed on earth, the naked soul
will seek refuge in Dis, and will correct
the cruel error of the blind Dealer
of destinies. And you, for whom long
unrequited love, and long faith,
and empty unfulfilled desire stirred
me to frenzy, live happy, if any mortal
ever lived happy on earth. Me, when
illusions and the dream of my childhood
perished, miserly Jove did not bless with
the sweet remedy for pain. Every one
of our happiest days is first to go.

Sottentra il morbo, e la vecchiezza, e l'ombra
della gelida morte. Ecco di tante
sperate palme, e dilettosi errori,
il Tartaro m'avanza; e il prode ingegno
han la tenaria Diva,
e l'atra notte, e la silente riva.

Disease and old age creep in, and the shadow
of frigid death. So, of all the many hoped-for
honors and sweet illusions only Tartarus remains
for me; and staunch genius the tenarian goddess
holds, the deep night and the silent shore.

COMMENTARY

It's very common today to find that a truly exceptional
and great man has an expressive face and lively eyes but that
the rest of his body is spare and thin and even deformed.
Think of Pope, Canova, Voltaire, Descartes, Pascal. The point
is this: the greatness connected with genius cannot be
achieved in our day without the soul wearing out the body,
like the sword wears out its sheath. It was different in antiq-
uity where genius and greatness were much more natural and
spontaneous and could develop without so many obstacles to
overcome; where the destructive cognition of truth (which
today goes hand in hand with great talent) was not as
powerful, where there was a greater concern with physical
exercise, which was considered to be a noble and necessary
activity and regarded as such even by men of great genius, like
Socrates, etc.

(Pensieri I, 8/10/1820)

The most terrible calamities in a person who — though
innocent and kind — is unattractive, as in the case of an old
and ugly man or woman, arouse in us only the most
indifferent kind of sympathy; . . . whereas only a few words
suffice to draw us to a young and beautiful woman, even if we
don't know her at all, and make us respond to a simple
account of some misfortune she has suffered. For this reason
we can continue to admire Socrates but never feel with him
completely; he is, in fact, the worst possible subject for
tragedy. And any novelist who would draw ugly and unfortu-
nate characters is on the wrong track. The same is true in the
case of a poet. Whatever the form of poetry he chooses to
write in, he must take great care not to suggest that he himself

47

might be ugly, for in reading a beautiful poem, we invariably imagine a beautiful poet. The contrast would be most unpleasant to the reader, especially if the poet talks about himself, describes his own misfortunes, his own unrequited love, as Petrarch and others do.

(Pensieri I, 8/21/1820)

A man who has imagination, enthusiasm, and feeling but does not have an attractive body is, with respect to nature, pretty much what the ardent and sincere lover — whose love is not returned — is with respect to his beloved. He rushes fervently toward nature, feels her power, her spell, her beauties, her many attractions profoundly, loves her to distraction; but like one whose love is not returned, he feels he can never be part of that beauty he loves and admires, that he must forever remain shut out, like the lover who is denied the heart, the tenderness, the company of his beloved. And the effort to examine those feelings about nature and beauty is always painful with respect to his own situation. He realizes immediately and repeatedly that the beauty which he admires, loves, and is drawn to does not belong to him. He experiences the same pain that one feels seeing or remembering the person one loves in another's arms, or that person in love with someone else and completely oblivious to your presence. He feels as though nature and beauty were not meant for him but for others; and — what is even more bitter — that those others are less worthy than he, in fact most unworthy, to enjoy beauty and nature, incapable of feeling and knowing her. He experiences the same disgust and the same excruciating pain that a starving man feels when he sees others dining on the most delicate food, eating well and enjoying it, knowing all the while that he will never have a chance to try it.

(Pensieri II, 3/5/1821)

What is beauty? Essentially the same thing as nobility and wealth: a gift of chance. Is a man of sensibilities and greatness less to be admired because he is not handsome? . . . And yet, the writer or poet must be careful not to depict him as ugly and avoid making comparisons about his looks. The whole effect would be lost if in talking about himself (as Petrarch does) or about his hero the author were to say that he was unlucky in love because his appearance, his aspect, his outward manner (which is wholly related to the body) were not attractive to the beloved, or because he was less handsome than a certain rival, etc. What indeed is the world other than *nature*? I have said that the human intellect is a material thing in its operation and conception. And this theory of the intellect must be applied to the emotions and the imagination. Virtue, feeling, the greatest moral values, the purest attributes of man — the most sublime, infinite, and furthest removed in appearance from matter — will not draw us, will have no effect whatsoever except as matter and material things. If you separate them from beauty or outward manner, they do not speak to us. We may fool ourselves in our hearts that we love the soul, or that we feel something more than matter; but it is an absolutely misleading notion.

(Pensieri III, 9/13/1821)

In his unhappy state, man understandably has a tendency to put the blame not on the nature of things or the human condition but (since he can't help blaming someone) always on a particular person or thing in which he finds relief for the bitterness caused by his ills as the proper object for his hatred and reproaches. For these would be much less satisfying than they are, to one who suffers, if they could not be directed toward someone who can assume the blame. This natural tendency works in such a way that the wretched man then convinces himself that all that he imagines is really so and even yearns for it to be true. Thus it is that his imagination has given shapes and names to *fortune* and *fate*, who for so long a time have been blamed for man's misfortunes and who were hated profoundly even by men of antiquity, and against whom — even in our day, in the absence of other possibilities — we hurl the most heartfelt hatred and reproaches for the ills we have to bear.

(Pensieri VI, 4/17/1824)

ALLA SUA DONNA
(1823)

Cara beltà che amore
lunge m'ispiri o nascondendo il viso,
fuor se nel sonno il core
ombra diva mi scuoti,
e ne' campi ove splenda
più vago il giorno e di natura il riso;
forse tu l'innocente
secol beasti che dall'oro ha nome,
or leve intra la gente
anima voli? O te la sorte avara
ch'a noi t'asconde, agli avvenir prepara?

Viva mirarti omai
nulla speme m'avanza;
s'allor non fosse, allor che ignudo e solo
per novo calle a peregrina stanza
verrà lo spirto mio. Già sul novello
aprir di mia giornata incerta e bruna,
te viatrice in questo arido suolo
io mi pensai. Ma non è cosa in terra
che ti somigli; e s'anco pari alcuna
ti fosse al volto, agli atti, alla favella,
saria, così conforme, assai men bella.

Fra cotanto dolore
quanto all'umana età propose il fato,
se vera e quale il mio pensier ti pinge,
alcun t'amasse in terra, a lui pur fôra
questo viver beato:
e ben chiaro vegg'io siccome ancora
seguir loda e virtù qual ne' prim'anni
l'amor tuo mi farebbe. Or non aggiunse

TO HIS LADY

Dear beauty that inspires love
in me from afar, or hiding your face,
except in sleep, or in the fields
where day and nature's smile
shine brighter, you stir my heart,
elusive goddess, did you perhaps
grace the innocent age that's known
as golden, now fly above us humans,
light spirit? or does grudging fate
that hides you from us, keep you
for others yet to come?

No hope is left me now to see you
in the flesh; if not, if not when
by a new path my spirit naked
and alone will reach the pilgrim's
resting place. Since the beginning
of my dark uncertain life, I pictured
you a voyager in this arid place.
But there is nothing on earth that
resembles you; and even if one appeared
to be like you in face, gestures,
in manner of speech, even so,
she would be much less beautiful than you.

Amid such pain as fate proposed
for humankind, if someone were
to love you here on earth, true and
such as my imagination pictures you,
this life for him would be heavenly:
and certainly I see clearly how
your love might still lead me to seek
out praise and virtue as it did in my
early days. But heaven did not add

51

il ciel nullo conforto ai nostri affanni;
e teco la mortal vita saria
simile a quella che nel ciel india.

   Per le valli, ove suona
del faticoso agricoltore il canto,
ed io seggo e mi lagno
del giovanil error che m'abbandona;
e per li poggi, ov'io rimembro e piagno
i perduti desiri, e la perduta
speme de' giorni miei; di te pensando,
a palpitar mi sveglio. E potess'io,
nel secol tetro e in questo aer nefando,
l'alta specie serbar; che dell'imago,
poi che del ver m'è tolto, assai m'appago.

   Se dell'eterne idee
l'una sei tu, cui sensibil forma
sdegni l'eterno senno esser vestita,
e fra caduche spoglie
provar gli affanni di funerea vita;
o s'altra terra ne' superni giri
fra' mondi innumerabili t'accoglie,
e più vaga del Sol prossima stella
t'irraggia, e più benigno etere spiri;
di qua dove son gli anni infausti e brevi,
questo d'ignoto amante inno ricevi.

any comfort to our miseries; and life
on earth with you would be like that
which makes us gods in heaven.

In the valleys, where the busy
farmer's song resounds, and I sit and
groan over the illusions of my youth
that now abandon me; and in the hills,
where I remember and grieve for desires
now spent, and for the lost hope of my
youth; thinking of you, I start up,
my heart pounding. And if in this
depressing age and this nefarious
atmosphere, I could preserve the lofty
vision; its likeness, since the true one
is denied me, is enough for me.

If you are one of the eternal notions,
that will not dress your eternal breast
with sensuous form, or take on among
short-lived pleasures the miseries of this
gloomy life; or if some other earth
among the countless worlds in the
furthest circles of outer space welcomes
you, and its nearest star shines on you
more brightly than the Sun, and a kinder
air is yours to breathe; from here,
where the years are brief and ill-fated,
accept this tribute from an unknown lover.

COMMENTARY

The most solid delight in this life of ours is the empty
delight of illusions. For me, illusions are in a sense very real,
since they constitute an essential ingredient of human nature
as a whole, which nature gives to each and every one of us, so
that they cannot be disparaged as the dreams of a single

person, but are clearly common to all men and as such the will of nature, and without which our life would be most wretched and barbarous.

(Pensieri I, 1819)

It doesn't take very long for our illusions to take hold of us again and win over the soul once more, even against our will. So long as he is alive, man without fail continues to hope for the happiness he has lost, he experiences that comfort which he was certain and had judged to be impossible, forgetting and discrediting the bitter truth that had taken root in his mind. The firmest, most complete and repeated disillusionment, though a daily experience, cannot resist the power of nature that forever brings back our false hopes and expectations.

(Pensieri I. 1/16/1821)

Years ago I was capable of the most furious passion . . . . I came very close to killing myself a number of times in my yearning for love, even though in reality the only reason for my despair was in my imagination.

(Epistolario I, to his cousin G. Melchiori. 12/19/1823)

I don't blame . . . anyone who is still seriously capable . . . of falling in love; on the contrary, I envy and congratulate him, because even though love is a pure figment and brings a great deal of suffering, it also brings with it a greater number of pleasures, and though it brings with it many ills, these are cancelled in the many delights that we enjoy,

(Epistolario I, to his cousin G. Melchiori. 2/2/1824)

I heard about a man who, every time he has a pleasant dream about the woman he loves, avoids her the next day and refuses to see her, knowing that she could never match the image of his dream and that seeing her in person would destroy the extraordinary pleasure of the "false" picture.

(Operette morali, "Dialogo di Torquato Tassso e del suo Genio.")

GIACOMO LEOPARDI

DIALOGO DI FEDERICO RUYSCH E DELLE SUE MUMMIE (1824)

Coro di morti nello studio di Federico Ruysch

Sola nel mondo eterna, a cui si volve
ogni creata cosa,
in te, morte, si posa,
nostra ignuda natura;
lieta no, ma sicura
dell'antico dolor. Profonda notte
nella confusa mente
il pensier grave oscura;
alla speme, al desio, l'arido spirto
lena mancar si sente:
così d'affanno e di temenza è sciolto,
e l'età vote e lente
senza tedio consuma.
Vivemmo: e qual paurosa larva,
e di sudato sogno,
a lattante fanciullo erra nell'alma
confusa ricordanza:
tal memoria n'avanza
del viver nostro: ma da tema è lunge
il rimembrar. Che fummo?
Che fu quel punto acerbo
che di vita ebbe nome?
Cosa arcana e stupenda
oggi è la vita al pensiero nostro, e tale
qual de' vivi al pensiero
l'ignota morte appar. Come da morte
vivendo rifuggia, così rifugge
dalla fiamma vitale
nostra ignuda natura;
lieta no ma sicura,

AN EXCHANGE BETWEEN FREDERICK RUYSCH* AND HIS MUMMIES

Chorus of the dead, in Frederick Ruysch's study

Alone eternal in the world,
to which all things created
turn, in you, death, our
naked being comes to rest;
not joyful, no, but safe from
the old pain. Deep night
hides all heavy thought
in the confused mind;
the withered spirit has no
strength left for hope, for desire:
so it is freed from burdens
and from fears, and wears away
the empty years without tedium.
We lived once: and just as
the confused memory of frightening
dreams and troubled sleep
recurs in the soul of an infant:
such is the memory we have
of our being alive: but fear is far
past remembering. Who were we?
what was that bitter point
that went by the name of life?
A strange and baffling thing
life seems to us today,
and unknown death appears
to the living in the same way.
Even as it flees from death,
while living, so our naked being
flees from the vital flame;
not joyful, no, but safe,

57

però ch'esser beato
nega ai mortali e nega a' morti il fato.

Ruysch (fuori dello studio, guardando per gli spiragli dell'uscio). Chi ha insegnato la musica a questi morti, che cantano di mezza notte come galli! In verità che io sudo freddo, e per poco non sono più morto di loro. Io non mi pensava perché gli ho preservati dalla corruzione, che mi risuscitassero. Tant'è: con tutta la filosofia, tremo da capo a piedi. Mal abbia quale diavolo che mi tentò di mettermi questa gente in casa. Non so che mi fare. Se gli lascio qui chiusi, che so che non rompano l'uscio, e non escano pel buco della chiave, e mi vengano a trovare al letto? Chiamare aiuto per paura de' morti, non mi sta bene. Via, facciamoci coraggio, e proviamo un poco di far paura a loro.

(Entrando). Figliuoli, a che giuoco giochiamo? Non vi ricordate di essere morti? Che è cotesto baccano? . . . . Io m'immagino che abbiate avuto intenzione di far da burla, e non da vero. Se siete risuscitati, me ne rallegro con voi; ma non ho tanto, he io possa far le spese ai vivi, come ai morti; e però levatevi di casa mia. Se è vero quel che si dice dei vampiri, e voi siete di quelli, cercate altro sangue da bere; che io non sono disposto a lasciarmi succhiare il mio, come vi sono stato liberale di quel finto, che vi ho messo nelle vene. In somma, se vorrete continuare a star quieti e in silenzio, come siete stati finora, resteremo in buona concordia, e in casa mia non vi mancherà niente, se no, avvertite ch'io piglio la stanga dell'uscio, e vi ammazzo tutti.

Morto. Non andare in collera; che io ti prometto che resteremo tutti morti come siamo, senza che tu ci ammazzi.

Ruysch. Dunque che è cotesta fantasia che vi è nata adesso, di cantare?

Morto. Poco fa sulla mezza notte appunto, si è compiuto per la prima volta quell'anno grande e matematico, di cui gli antichi scrivono tante cose; e questa similmente è la

for fate denies to the living and denies
to the dead their being happy.

Ruysch (outside his laboratory, peering through the keyhole).
Who's been giving music lessons to these dead, who sing
like roosters in the middle of the night? Truth is, I'm in a
cold sweat, almost more dead than they are! I never
thought they would come back to life because I saved them
from rotting away! Truth is: with all my learning, I can't
stop trembling from head to foot! May that devil who
tempted me to bring these people into my house come to
no good. I don't know what I should do. If I leave them
locked up, what if they break down the door or come
through the keyhole and visit me in my bed? For me to call
for help because I fear the dead doesn't sit right. Come on,
let's pull ourself together, and try to put some fear in *them.*
(Entering). Dear children, what kind of game are we
playing? Don't you remember you're dead? What's all this
racket? . . . . I imagine you wanted to play a joke, nothing
serious. If you've come back to life, I'm happy for you; but
I don't have enough to pay for the expenses of the living as
I have for the dead; and so, get out of my house. If it's true
what they say about vampires, and you are of their kind,
find other blood to drink; for I'm not ready to have you
suck mine in the same way I was generous with that fake
one I put in your veins. Listen here, if you continue to be
quiet and remain silent, as you have been until now, we'll
still get along, and you'll lack nothing in my house; if not,
let me warn you, I'll take the iron cross bar from the door
and kill you all.
Dead Man. Don't get youself all worked up, for I promise
you, we'll all stay dead, just as we are, without your having
to kill us.
Ruysch. So, what's this whim that's come over you just
now, to sing?
Dead Man. A little while ago, at midnight to be exact, the
great mathematical cycle about which the ancients wrote so

59

prima volta che i morti parlano. E non solo noi, ma in ogni cimitero, in ogni sepolcro, giù nel fondo del mare, sotto la neve o la rena, a cielo aperto, e in qualunque luogo si trovano, tutti i morti, sulla mezza notte, hanno cantato come noi quella canzoncina che hai sentita.

Ruysch. E quanto dureranno a cantare o a parlare?

Morto. Di cantare hanno già finito. Di parlare hanno facoltà per un quarto d'ora. Poi tornano in silenzio per insino a tanto che si compie di nuovo lo stesso anno.

Ruysch. Se cotesto è vero, non credo che mi abbiate a rompere il sonno un'altra volta. Parlate pure insieme liberamente; che io me ne starò qui da parte, e vi ascolterò volentieri, per curiosità, senza disturbarvi.

Morto. Non possiamo parlare altrimenti, che rispondendo a qualche persona viva. Chi non ha da replicare ai vivi, finita che ha la canzone, si accheta.

Ruysch. Mi dispiace veramente: perché m'immagino che sarebbe un gran sollazzo a sentire quello che vi direste fra voi, se poteste parlare insieme.

Morto. Quando anche potessimo, non sentiresti nulla; perché non avremmo che ci dire.

Ruysch. Mille domande da farvi mi vengano in mente. Ma perché il tempo ê corto, e non lascia luogo a scegliere, datemi ad intendere in ristretto, che sentimenti provaste di corpo e d'animo nel punto della morte.

Morto. Del punto proprio della morte, io non me ne accorsi.

Gli altri morti. Né anche noi.

Ruysch. Come non ve n'accorgeste?

Morto. Verbigrazia, come tu non ti accorgi mai del momento che tu cominci a dormire, per quanta attenzione ci vogli porre.

Ruysch. Ma l'addormentarsi è cosa naturale.

Morto. E il morire non ti pare naturale? mostrami un uomo, o una bestia, o una pianta, che non muoia.

Ruysch. Non mi maraviglio più che andiate cantando e parlando, se non vi accorgeste di morire.

much came to full circle for the first time; and this too is the first time the dead speak. And not just us, but in every cemetery, in every tomb, down at the bottom of the sea, under snow or sand, under open skies, wherever they find themselves, all the dead, at midnight, have sung, as we just did, that little song you just heard.

Ruysch. And how long will they go on singing or talking?

Dead Man. They are done singing. They are able to go on talking for fifteen minutes. After that, they fall silent until the same year comes around again.

Ruysch. If this is true, I don't think you'll get to disturb my sleep again. Please, talk freely among yourselves; I'll just stand here to one side and listen, out of curiosity, without bothering you.

Dead Man. We can't talk except in answer to a living person. Those who don't have to answer the living will fall silent once they have finished their song.

Ruysch. I'm truly sorry because I imagine it would be quite entertaining to hear what you would have to say to one another, if you could speak among yourselves.

Dead Man. Even if we could, you would hear nothing; for we have nothing to say to one another.

Ruysch. A thousand questions come to mind to ask you. But since time is short and doesn't leave much room for choice, explain to me briefly what feelings you experienced in your body and in your soul at the moment of death.

Dead Man. I was not aware of the exact moment of death.

The Other Dead Men. Nor were we.

Ruysch. What do you mean, you weren't aware of it?

Dead Man. Just as you, for instance, are never aware of the moment you begin to fall asleep, no matter how hard you try.

Ruysch. But falling asleep is natural.

Dead Man. And dying doesn't seem natural? Show me a man, a beast, a plant that doesn't die.

Ruysch. I'm no longer surprised at your singing and talking, seeing as how you weren't aware of dying.

Così colui, del colpo non accorto,
andava combattendo, ed era morto, **

dice un poeta italiano. Io mi pensava che sopra questa faccenda della morte, i vostri pari ne sapessero qualche cosa più che i vivi. Ma dunque, tornando sul sodo, non sentiste nessun dolore in punto di morte?

Morto. Che dolore ha da essere quello del quale chi lo prova, non se ne accorge?

Ruysch. A ogni modo, tutti si persuadono che il sentimento della morte sia dolorosissimo.

Morto. Quasi che la morte fosse un sentimento, e non piuttosto il contrario.

Ruysch. E tanto quelli che intorno alla natura dell'anima si accostano col parere delli Epicurei, quanto quelli che tengono la sentenza comune, tutti, o la più parte, concorrono in quello ch'io dico; cioè nel credere che la morte sia per natura propria, e senza nessuna comparazione, un dolore vivissimo.

Morto. Or bene, tu domanderai da nostra parte agli uni e agli altri: se l'uomo non ha facoltà di avvedersi del punto in cui le operazioni vitali, in maggior o minor parte, gli restano non più che interrotte, o per sonno o per letargo o per sincope o per qualunque cosa; come si avvedrà di quello in cui le medesime operazioni cessano del tutto, e non per poco spazio di tempo, ma in perpetuo? Oltre di ciò, come può essere che un sentimento vivo abbia luogo nella morte? anzi, che la stessa morte sia per propria qualità un sentimento vivo? Quando la facoltà di sentire è, non solo debilitata e scarsa, ma ridotta a cosa tanto minima, che ella manca e si annulla, credete voi che la persona sia capace di un sentimento forte? anzi questo medesimo estinguersi della facoltà di sentire, credete che debba essere un sentimento grandissimo? Vedete pure che anche quelli che muoiono di mali acuti e dolorosi, in sull'appressarsi della morte, più o meno tempo avanti dello spirare, si quietano e si riposano in modo, che si può conoscere che la loro vita, ridotta a piccola quantità, non è più

So he, not knowing that he bled,
Kept fighting, and all the while was dead,**
as an Italian poet wrote. I was under the impression that
you people would know a bit more than the living about
this business of dying. But now, coming back to our
subject, you felt no pain at the moment of death?

Dead Man. What pain can it be that the one who
experiences it is not aware of it?

Ruysch. In any case, everyone seems persuaded that the
feeling of death is most painful.

Dead Man. As though death were a feeling, instead of the
opposite.

Ruysch. Both those who follow the opinion of the
Epicureans with regard to the nature of the soul and those
who hold the common view, all, or most of them, agree
with what I say; that is, that death is by its very nature, and
without possibile comparison, the sharpest pain.

Dead Man. Fine, then ask both those and the others, for
us: if man is incapable of noticing the moment in which the
vital functions are to a greater or lesser extent interrupted,
whether by sleep or lethargy, or a stroke, or whatever
reason, how will he know when those same functions cease
completely, and not for a short period of time, but forever?
Besides which, how can a sharp feeling be part of death? in
fact, how can death itself by its very nature be a sharp
feeling? When the ability to experience is not only
weakened and greatly diminished but reduced to such a
point that it fails and then ceases altogether, do you think a
person is capable of strong feeling? better yet, do you think
this same extinguishing of the ability to experience has to
be an ovewhelming feeling? You see, also, that even those
who die from terrible and painful illnesses grow quiet and
relaxed as death draws near, at some time more or less
before breathing their last, so that one can see their life,
reduced to a small fraction, no longer registers pain, and
so this ceases before the other. Tell them that much, for us,
those who believe they will have to die suffering at the

sufficiente al dolore, sicché questo cessa prima di quella. Tanto dirai da parte nostra a chiunque si pensa di avere a morir di dolore in punto di morte.

Ruysch. Agli Epicurei forse potranno bastare coteste ragioni. Ma non a quelli che giudicano altrimenti della sostanza dell'anima; come ho fatto io per lo passato, e farò da ora inanzi molto maggiormente, avendo udito parlare e cantare i morti. Perché stimando che il morire consista in una separazione dell'anima dal corpo, non comprenderanno come queste due cose, congiunte e quasi conglutinate tra loro in modo, che constituiscono l'una e l'altra una sola persona, si possano separare senza una grandissima violenza, e un travaglio indicibile.

Morto. Dimmi: lo spirito è forse appiccato al corpo con qualche nervo, o con qualche muscolo o membrana, che di necessità si abbia a rompere quando lo spirito si parte? o forse è un membro del corpo, in modo che n'abbia a essere schiantato o reciso violentemente? Non vedi che l'anima in tanto esce di esso corpo, in quando solo è impedita di rimanervi, e non v'ha più luogo; non già per nessuna forza che ne la strappi e sradichi? Dimmi ancora: forse nell'entrarvi, ella vi si sente conficcare o allacciare gagliardamente, o come tu dici, conglutinare? Perché dunque sentirà spiccarsi all'uscirne, o vogliamo dire proverà una sensazione veementissima? Abbi per fermo, che l'entrata e l'uscita dell'anima sono parimente quiete, facili e molli.

Ruysch. Dunque, che cosa è la morte, se non è dolore?

Morto. Piuttosto piacere che altro. Sappi che il morire, come l'addormentarsi, non si fa in un solo istante, ma per gradi. Vero è che questi gradi sono più o meno, o maggiori o minori, secondo la varietà delle cause e dei generi della morte. Nell'ultimo di tali istanti la morte non reca né dolore né piacere alcuno, come né anche il sonno. Negli altri precedenti non può generare dolore perché il dolore è cosa viva, e i sensi dell'uomo in quel tempo, cioè cominciata che è la morte, sono moribondi, che è quanto

moment of death.

Ruysch. The Epicureans may be satisfied with such reasonings. But not those who think differently about the substance of the soul, as I have for a long time and will even more from this moment on, having heard the dead talk and sing! Because, believing that dying is the separation of the soul from the body, they won't be able to grasp how those two things, held together, glued almost to each other in such a way that one and the other form a single person, can come apart without tremendous violence and indescribable effort.

Dead Man. Tell me: is the soul stuck to the body by some nerve maybe, or some muscle or membrane that must be broken when the soul leaves? or maybe it's a limb of the body, so that it has to be chopped off, cut away violently? Don't you see that the soul leaves the body only when it is prevented from remaining in it and has no place there any more; never because it is wrenched away and uprooted by some great force? Tell me further: on entering, does it feel itself pushed in, maybe, or tied up tightly, or as you say, glued on? Why then will it feel itself being torn away when leaving, or, let us say, experience a most violent sensation? Rest assured that the coming and going of the soul are equally quiet, easy, and gentle.

Ruysch. So then, what is death, if it isn't pain?

Dead Man. Pleasure, rather than anything else. Keep in mind that dying, like falling asleep, doesn't happen in a single moment but by degrees. It's true that these degrees are more or less, greater or smaller, depending on the various causes and kinds of death. In the very last of these moments, death brings on neither pain nor pleasure of any kind, any more than sleep does. In the ones preceding this, it cannot generate pain, because pain is something sharp and a person's senses at such a time, that is, once death has taken hold, are ebbing, which is to say, extremely diminished in strength. It may actually generate pleasure: because pleasure is not always something sharp; in fact, the

dire estremamente attenuati di forze. Può bene esser causa di piacere: perché il piacere non sempre è cosa viva; anzi forse la maggior parte dei diletti umani consistono in qualche sorta di languidezza. Di modo che i sensi del'uomo sono capaci di piacere anche presso all'estinguersi; atteso che spessissime volte la stessa languidezza è piacere; massime quando vi libera da patimento; poiché ben sai che la cessazione di qualunque dolore o disagio, è piacere per se medesima. Sicché il languore della morte debbe essr più grato secondo che libera l'uomo da maggior patimento. Per me, se bene nell'ora della morte non posi molta attenzione a quel che io sentiva, perché mi era proibito dai medici di affaticare il cervello; mi ricordo però che il senso che provai, non fu molto dissimile dal diletto che è cagionato agli uomini dal languore del sonno, nel tempo che si vengono addormentando.

Gli altri morti. Anche a noi pare di ricordarci altrettanto.

Ruysch. Sia come voi dite: benché tutti quelli coi quali ho avuta occasione di ragionare sopra questa materia, giudicavano molto diversamente: ma, che io mi ricordi, non allegavano la loro esperienza propria. Ora ditemi: nel tempo della morte, mentre sentivate quella dolcezza, vi credeste di morire, e che quel diletto fosse una cortesia della morte; o pure immaginaste qualche altra cosa?

Morto. Finché non fui morto, non mi persuasi mai di non avere a scampare di quel pericolo; e se non altro, fino all'ultimo punto che ebbi facoltà di pensare, sperai che mi avanzasse di vita un'ora o due: come stimo che succeda a molti, quando muoiono.

Gli altri morti. A noi successe il medesimo.

Ruysch. Così Cicerone dice che nessuno è talmente decrepito, che non si prometta di vivere almanco un anno. Ma come vi accorgeste in ultimo, che lo spirito era uscito dal corpo? Dite: come conosceste d'essere morti? Non rispondono. Figliuoli, non m'intendete? Sarà passato il quarto d'ora. Tastiamogli un poco. Sono rimorti ben bene: non è pericolo che mi abbiano da far paura un'altra volta:

greater part of human joys consists of some kind of languor. So that a person's senses are capable of pleasure even as they near extinction; once it is understood that very often languor itself is a pleasure; especially when it frees you from pain, since, as you well know, the end of any kind of pain or discomfort is in itself pleasure. So the languor of death must be the more welcome to the extent that it frees man from a greater suffering. As for me, although I wasn't paying much attention to what I was feeling at the time of my death, for the doctors had forbidden me to tax my brain, I do recall that the feeling I experienced was not much different from the delight that comes to all men from the languor of sleep, as they begin to drift off.

The Other Dead Men. We seem to remember something like that too.

Ruysch. If you say so, although all those I've ever had occasion to talk with about the matter had very different opinions: but, as I recall, they did not speak from personal experience. So, tell me now: at the time of death, as you felt that sweetness, did you think you were dying, and that such delight was a courtesy extended by death, or did you imagine something else?

Dead Man. Until I was dead, I never believed I couldn't escape that danger; and, if nothing else, until the last moment that I retained my faculty to think, I hoped for one or two more hours of life, as I imagine happens to many others when they die.

The Other Dead Men. The same happened to us.

Ruysch. That's what Cicero says, that no one is so decrepit that he doesn't believe he has at least one more year to live. But how did you become aware at the end, that the soul had left the body? Tell me, how did you realize that you were dead? They're not answering. My children, can't you hear me? The fifteen minutes must be up. Let's poke them a little. They're dead, again, for sure: no way they can frighten me again: back to bed, then.

torniamocene a letto.

*A Dutch medical doctor and naturalist (1638-1731), famous in his day for having found a way to embalm bodies so that they seemed very much alive.

**From Francesco Berni's version of M. M. Boiardo's, Orlando innamorato, Canto 53, st. 60. (My translation.)

AL CONTE CARLO PEPOLI
(1826)

Questo affannoso e travagliato sonno
che noi vita nomian, come sopporti,
Pepoli mio? di che speranze il core
vai sostenendo? in che pensieri, in quanto
o gioconde o moleste opre dispensi
l'ozio che ti lasciâr gli avi remoti,
grave retaggio e faticoso? È tutta,
in ogni umano stato, ozio la vita,
se quell'oprar, quel procurar che a degno
obbietto non intende, o che all'intento
giunger mai non potria, ben si conviene
ozioso nomar. La schiera industre
cui franger glebe o curar piante e greggi
vede l'alba tranquilla e vede il vespro,
se oziosa dirai, da che sua vita
è per campar la vita, e per sé sola
la vita all'uomo non ha pregio nessuno,
dritto e vero dirai. Le notti e i giorni
tragge in ozio il nocchiero; ozio il perenne
sudar nelle officine, ozio le vegghie
son de' guerrieri e il perigliar nell'armi;
e il mercatante avaro in ozio vive:
che non a sé, non ad altrui, la bella
felicità, cui solo agogna e cerca
la natura mortal, veruno acquista
per cura o per sudor, veggia o periglio.
Pure all'aspro desire onde i mortali
già sempre infin dal dì che il mondo nacque
d'esser beati sospirâr indarno,
di medicina in loco apparechiate
nella vita infelice avea natura
necessità diverse, a cui non senza

TO COUNT CARLO PEPOLI

This wearing and oppressive sleep
that we call life, how do you bear it,
my Pepoli? with what hopes do you
sustain your heart? with what thoughts,
what pleasant or oppressive cares
do you fill the idle leisure bequeathed
to you by remote forbears, a difficult
and heavy legacy? All life, in every human
state, is idle effort, if striving not aimed
at worthy goals, or aimed at goals
that never can be reached, is rightly to be
called idle. Were you to call idle
the industrious crowd that quiet dawn
and evening see breaking rocks
or tending crops and herds, you would
be saying what's right and true,
since life for them is to get through this life,
and in itself life is no boon to man.
In idle effort, the helmsman ferries
his nights and days; idle effort
the endless sweating in workshops;
idle effort are the soldier's watches,
and the risks of battle; and the greedy
merchant lives in idle effort: for no one
can win either for himself or others,
by care or sweat, watches or risks,
that lovely happiness, the only thing that
mortal nature longs for and pursues.
Yet, to counter the keen longing
to be happy, which man has vainly
yearned for ever since the world
was born, nature provided remedies
along the way, various needs
that must be met, in this sorry life,

opra e pensier si provvedesse, e pieno,
poi che lieto non può, coresse il giorno
all'umana famiglia; onde agitato
e confuso il desio, men loco avesse
al travagliarne il cor. Così de' bruti
la progenie infinita, a cui pur solo,
né men vano che a noi, vive nel petto
desio d'esser beati; e quello intenta
che a lor vita è mestier, di noi men tristo
condur si scopre e men gravoso il tempo,
né la lentezza accagionar dell'ore.
Ma noi, che il viver nostro all'altrui mano
provveder commettiamo, una più grave
necessità, cui provveder non puote
altri che noi, già senza tedio e pena
non adempiam: necessitate, io dico,
di consumar la vita: improba, invitta
necessità, cui non tesoro accolto,
non di greggi dovizia, o pingui campi,
non aula puote e non purpureo manto
sottrar l'umana prole. Or s'altri, a sdegno
i vòti anni prendendo, e la superna
luce odiando, l'omicida mano,
i tardi fati a prevenir condotto,
in se stesso non torce; al duro morso
della brama insanabile che invano
felicità richiede, esso da tutti
lati cercando, mille inefficaci
medicine procaccia, onde quell'una
cui natura apprestò, mal si compensa.

Lui delle vesti e delle chiome il culto
e degli atti e dei passi, e i vani studi
di cocchi e di cavalli, e le frequenti
sale, e le piazze romorose, e gli orti,
lui giochi e cene e invidiate danze
tengon la notte e il giorno; a lui dal labbro

not without planning and hard work,
so that the day, which for the human
family could never be a happy one,
might be at least a full one, and so
their yearning, struggling and confused,
have less space in which to wring the heart.
So is it with the endless progeny of brutes
who also nurture, no less vainly than do we,
the one desire to be happy; and concentrating
on the daily business of their lives,
they find the going easier than we do,
time less oppressive, nor complain about
the hours dragging. But we who commit
to other hands provision for our lives must
take on, not without pain and tedium,
a greater charge, one that no other being
can be entrusted with: I mean, the charge
to see life through: a crushing, inescapable
charge, from which no store of riches,
no wealth of flocks or herds or fertile fields,
no palace or royal mantle can free the human
race. Now, if someone, scorning the empty
years and hating heaven's light, led to
anticipate the sluggish fates, does not
turn his homicidal hand upon himself;
at the hard pull of the unhealable desire
that seeks happiness in vain, he turns
everywhere, searching, tries thousands of
ineffectual remedies, yet gives poor credit
to the one nature was quick to provide.

    This one follows fashions of dress and hair,
gestures and gait, the empty pursuit of horses
and carriages, social gatherings, noisy crowds,
garden parties, games and dinners, and
fashionable balls keep this one busy night
and day; a smile is never absent from his lips;

mai non si parte il riso; ahi, ma nel petto,
nell'imo petto, grave, salda, immota
come colonna adamantina, siede
noia immortale, incontro a cui non puote
vigor di giovanezza, e non la crolla
dolce parola di rosato labbro,
e non lo sgardo tenero, tremante,
di due nere pupille, il caro sgardo
la più degna del ciel cosa mortale.

    Altri, quasi a fuggir vòlto la trista
umana sorte, in cangiar terre e climi
l'età spendendo, e mari e poggi errando,
tutto l'orbe trascorre, ogni confine
degli spazi che all'uom negl'infiniti
campi del tutto la natura aperse,
peregrinando aggiunge. Ahi ahi, s'asside
su l'alte prue la negra cura, e sotto
ogni clima, ogni ciel, si chiama indarno
felicità, vive tristezza e regna.

    Havvi che le crudeli opre di marte
sí elegge a passar l'ore, e nel fraterno
sangue la man tinge per ozio; ed havvi
che d'altrui danni si conforta, e pensa
con far misero altrui far sé men tristo,
sì che nocendo usar procaccia il tempo.
E chi virtute o sapienza ed arti
perseguitando; e chi la propria gente
conculcando e l'estrane, o di remoti
lidi turbando le quiete antica
col mercatar, con l'armi, e con le frodi,
la destinata sua vita consuma.

    Te più mite desio, cura più dolce
regge nel fior di gioventù, nel bello
april degli anni, altrui giocondo e primo

ah, but deep inside, deep down inside, heavy,
somber, and unmovable, like an adamantine
column, sits immortal tedium, impervious
to the strength of youth, unshaken by sweet
words from rosy lips, or by the tender trembling
glance of two dark eyes, that dear glance,
the one mortal thing most worthy of heaven.

   Another, as if bent on fleeing the sorry lot
of man, spending his time moving through
different lands and climes, and wandering
over seas and mountains, crosses the entire globe,
takes in, traveling, every last corner of space
in the all-encompassing infinite stretches
that nature opened to man. Ah, ah, black care
takes its seat on the high prow, and
under every sky, every climate, happiness
in vain is invoked, sorrow lives and reigns.

   There are those who choose to pass the
hours in cruel works of Mars, and in their
idle effort stain their hands in brother's
blood, and there are those who find comfort
in the ills of others, and think, by making
others miserable, to make themselves less
sad, so that their time is spent in hurting
others. And some, in persecuting virtue
or wisdom, or the arts; and those who
spend their whole lives putting down
their own people and those abroad, or
disrupting the long-standing peace of far-off
shores with trade or arms or treachery.

   A milder wish and sweeter care sustain
you, in the flower of your youth, the lovely
april of our years, for others, heaven's joyful
and greatest gift, but heavy, bitter,

dono del ciel, ma grave, amaro, infesto
a chi patria non ha. Te punge e move
studio de' carmi e di ritrar parlando
il bel che raro e scarso e fuggitivo
appar nel mondo, e quel che più benigna
di natura e del ciel, fecondamente
a noi la vaga fantasia produce
e il nostro proprio error. Ben mille volte
fortunato colui che la caduca
virtù del caro immaginar non perde
per volger d'anni; a cui serbare eterna
la gioventù del cor diedero i fati;
che nella ferma e nella stanca etade,
così come solea nell'età verde,
in suo chiuso pensier natura abbella,
morte, deserto avviva. A te conceda
tanta ventura il ciel; ti faccia un tempo
la favilla che il petto oggi ti scalda,
di poesia canuto amante. Io tutti
della prima stagione i dolci inganni
mancar già sento, e dileguar dagli occhi
le dilettose immagini, che tanto
amai, che sempre infino all'ora estrema
mi fieno, a ricordar, bramate e piante.
Or quando al tutto irrigidito e freddo
questo petto sarà, né dagli aprichi
campi il sereno e solitario riso,
né degli augelli mattutini il canto
di primavera, né per colli e piagge
sotto limpido ciel tacita luna
commoverammi il cor; quando mi fia
ogni beltate o di natura o d'arte,
fatta inanime e muta; ogni alto senso,
ogni tenero affetto, ignoto e strano;
del mio solo conforto allor mendico,
altri studi men dolci, in ch'io riponga
l'ingrato avanzo della ferrea vita,

tainted to one who has no country.
You the study of poetry prods and moves,
and painting with words the beautiful
which rare and fleeting and short-lived
appears on earth, and what our restless
imagination, and our own illusions, kinder
than nature or heaven, produce in profusion.
Blessed a thousand times is he who with
the passing years does not lose the fleeting
power of his dear fantasizing; to whom
the fates allowed that he remain forever
young at heart; so that in his sick and weary
age, as he was wont to do when young,
he beautifies nature in his mind, gives life
to death and desert. May heaven grant you
such a future; may the spark which kindles
your heart today, turn you, in time,
into a white-haired lover of poetry.
I feel the sweet illusions of my early days
all slip away already, and the delightful
images I loved so much, that remembering,
will always be craved and lamented
to my dying hour, fade from my eyes.
Then when to all things this breast
will have grown stiff and cold,
and the serene and solitary smile
of open fields, the early morning song
of birds in spring, the silent moon
above the hills and valleys in a limpid
sky no longer move my heart,
when every beauty of nature or of art
becomes still and mute for me, every lofty
feeling, every tender emotion strange
and alien; deprived then of my only
solace, I will in other studies, less sweet,
elect to spend the wretched
remnant of this hard existence.

eleggerò. L'acerbo vero, i ciechi
destini investigar delle mortali
e dell'eterne cose; a che prodotta,
a che d'affanni e di miserie carca
l'umana stirpe; a quale ultimo intento
lei spinga il fato e la natura; a cui
tanto nostro dolor diletti o giovi:
con quali ordini e leggi a che si volva
questo arcano universo; il qual di lode
colmano i saggi, io d'ammirar son pago.

In questo specolar gli ozi traendo
verrò: che conosciuto, ancor che tristo,
ha suoi diletti il vero. E se del vero
ragionando talor, fieno alle genti
o mal grati i miei detti o non intesi,
non mi dorrò, che già del tutto il vago
desio di gloria antico in me fia spento:
vana Diva non pur, ma di fortuna
e del fato e d'amor, Diva più cieca.

I will search out the bitter truth,
the blind destinies of mortal and
eternal things; for what reason
the human race was made
for what reason burdened with
suffering and pain; to what ultimate
purpose it is driven by nature or fate;
who might find profit and joy
in all this suffering of ours;
where, and by what rules and laws,
this arcane universe is tending;
which the learned heap with praise,
I am content just to admire.

In such speculation I'll go on dragging
my idle tasks, for, once known, though sad,
the truth has pleasures of its own.
And if in speaking of the truth at times,
my words prove less than welcome
to people, or are misconstrued, I will
not be offended; for the old restless wish
for fame is now entirely spent in me:
not just an empty Deity, but a Deity more
blind than fortune, than fate, than love.

A SILVIA
(1828)

Silvia, rimembri ancora
quel tempo della tua vita mortale,
quando beltà splendea
negli occhi tuoi ridenti e fuggitivi,
e tu, lieta e pensosa, il limitare
di gioventù salivi?

   Sonavan le quiete
stanze, e le vie dintorno,
al tuo perpetuo canto,
allor che all'opre femminili intenta
sedevi, assai contenta
di quel vago avvenir che in mente avevi.
Era il maggio odoroso: e tu solevi
così menare il giorno.

   Io gli studi leggiadri
talor lasciando e le sudate carte,
ove il tempo mio primo
e di me si spendea la miglior parte,
d'in su i veroni del paterno ostello
porgea gli orecchi sl suon della tua voce,
ed alla man veloce
che percorrea la faticosa tela.
Mirava il ciel sereno,
le vie dorate e gli orti,
e quinci il mar da lungi, e quindi il monte.
Lingua mortal non dice
Quel ch'io sentiva in seno.

   Che pensieri soavi,
che speranze, che cori, o Silvia mia!

TO SILVIA

Sylvia, do you still remember
that time in your mortal life
when beauty shone in your elusive
and smiling eyes, and you,
thoughtful and happy, climbed
the threshold of your youth?

The quiet rooms and all the
streets around rang with your
constant singing while you sat,
intent on woman's work,
content with the pleasant future
pictured in your mind. It was
the fragrant month of May: and you
would spend your days this way.

At times, leaving my pleasant
studies and the worn pages
over which my early years
and the best of me were
being spent, I'd turn my ears
up to the terraces of my father's
house at the sound of your voice
and of your swift hand
working the heavy loom.
I'd gaze at the clear sky, the golden
streets, the gardens close by,
and on this side, the sea in the distance,
and on that side, the mountain.
Mortal tongue cannot
describe what I felt inside.

What sweet thoughts, what hopes,
what throbbing hearts, my Sylvia!

Quale allor ci apparia
la vita umana e il fato!
Quando sovviemmi di cotanta speme,
un affetto mi preme
acerbo a sconsolato,
e tornami a doler di mia sventura.
O natura, o natura,
perché non rendi poi
quel che prometti allor? perché di tanto
inganni i flgli tuoi?

Tu pria che l'erbe inaridisse il verno,
da chiuso morbo combattuta e vinta,
perivi, o tenerella. E non vedevi
il fior degli anni tuoi;
non ti molceva il core
la dolce lode or delle negre chiome,
or degli sguardi innamorati e schivi;
né teco le compagne ai dì festivi
ragionavan d'amore.

Anche peria fra poco
la speranza mia dolce: agli anni miei
anche negâro I fati
la giovanezza. Ahi, come,
come passata sei,
cara compagna dell'età mia nova,
mia lacrimata speme!
Questo è quel mondo? questi
i diletti, l'amor, l'opre, gli eventi
onde cotanto ragionammo insieme?
questa la sorte dell'umane genti?
All'appar del vero
tu, misera, cadesti: e con la mano
la fredda morte ed una tomba ignuda
mostravi di lontano.

What human life and fate seemed like,
back then! When I'm reminded
of all that hope a desolate and bitter
feeling takes hold of me, and once again
I mourn my wretched fate.
Oh nature, oh nature,
why don't you render later,
what you promise early on?
Why do you so betray your children?

Long before winter withered
the grass, you died, oh tender child,
consumed and conquered by some hidden
malady. And you did not see
the flower of your years; your heart
did not melt at sweet praise of your
dark hair, at shy smitten glances;
nor did the other girls, on the holiday,
get to talk with you about love.

My sweet hope, soon after,
also died: the fates denied my years
their youth, also. Oh, how quickly, how
quickly you went by, dear friend of my
young age, my long-mourned hope!
Is this that world? these the joys,
the love, the tasks, events, we talked
so much about, together?
this the destiny of man? At the sight
of the truth you fell, poor wretch,
and with your hand pointed, far off,
to a cold death and a bare tomb.

COMMENTARY

A woman of twenty, twenty-five, thirty, is apt to have
more power of attraction, a more experienced way about her,

and will inspire and, especially continue to keep alive, passion for her . . . . Still, a girl of sixteen or eighteen has in her face, her gestures, her voice, her steps, etc., something divine that nothing else can approximate. Whatever her character may be, her taste, whether she be merry or sad, serious or whimsical, lively or retiring, that purest, freshest untouched flower of youth, that whole and virgin hope mirrored in her face and actions which one sees in and through her, a certain air of innocence and inexperience of evil, of misfortunes, of suffering, that flower, I say, produces such a profound, ineffable, lively impression that — without falling in love or even having any lasting interest in her — one never tires of looking at her. I know of nothing else that can lift our soul, take us into another world, give us a taste of angels, heaven, divinity, happiness. All of this, as I said, without falling in love, without any desire to possess her . . . . Moreover, if we add to what I have already said about seeing and enjoying the sight of a girl of sixteen or eighteen, the realization of the sorrows awaiting her, the misfortunes that all too soon must darken and stifle that pure joy, the emptiness of all those treasured hopes, the brief bloom of that flower, that condition, all that beauty; and if we add our own familiar brooding to all his, and with it a deep compassion for that angel of happiness, for ourselves, for our human destiny, for life itself (all the things that inevitably must come to mind), we're bound to feel the most precious and sublime emotion imaginable.

(Pensieri VII, Florence. 6/30/1828)

To lose a person one loves by sudden accident or a brief and fatal illness is less bitter than to see that person failing day by day . . . because of a long sickness that transforms the body and soul even before the end comes, so that the person we knew seems unrecognizable to us. A terribly sad thing; because in this case the loved one doesn't simply disappear, . . . leaving behind the image we treasure in our soul . . . but instead the reality is fixed in our sight and it is altogether different from what we knew and loved before, so that all dreams of love are torn violently from us.

(Operette morali, "Detti memorabili di F. Ottonieri," cap. III)

THE LEOPARDI RESIDENCE

IL PASSARO SOLITARIO
(ca. 1828)

D'in su la vetta della torre antica,
passero solitario, alla campagna
cantando vai finchè non more il giorno;
ed erra l'armonia per questa valle.
Primavera dintorno
brilla nell'aria, e per li campi esulta,
sì ch'a mirarla intenerisce il core.
Odi greggi belar, muggire armenti;
gli altri augelli contenti, a gara insieme
per lo libero ciel fan mille giri,
pur festeggiando il lor tempo migliore:
tu pensoso in disparte il tutto miri;
non compagni, non voli,
non ti cal d'allegria, schivi gli spassi;
canti, e così trapassi
dell'anno e di tua vita il più bel fiore.

  Oimè, quanto somiglia
al tuo costume il mio! Sollazzo e riso,
della novella età dolce famiglia,
e te german di giovinezza, amore,
sospiro acerbo de' provetti giorni,
non curo, io non so come; anzi da loro
quasi fuggo lontano;
quasi romito, e strano
al mio loco natio,
passo del viver mio la primavera.
Questo giorno ch'omai cede alla sera,
festeggiar si costuma al nostro borgo.
Odi per lo sereno un suon di squilla,
odi spesso un tonar di ferree canne,
che rimbomba lontan di villa in villa.

THE SOLITARY SPARROW

From the summit of the old tower
you keep singing into the countryside,
solitary sparrow, until the day is spent;
and the sweet sound drifts across this
valley. Spring sparkles in the air
around, and rejoices in the fields,
so that the heart grows tender,
watching. You hear flocks bleating,
herds lowing; the other birds happy,
circle the open sky together
a thousand times, they too celebrating
their best season: you, thoughtful,
apart, watch it all; you care nothing
for fun-loving mates or flights,
scorn all play; you sing, and in this
way you move through the loveliest
bloom of the year and of your life.

Alas, how much your habits
are like mine! I care not, I don't
know why, for laughter and play,
sweet familiars of a tender age,
nor for you, love, brother of youth,
bitter memory of impressionable
days; in fact, I run from them, almost;
live out the springtime of my life,
a wanderer almost, and alien
to my own native place.
This day now turning into dusk,
has always been a holiday for us.
You hear sound of bells in the clear sky,
you often hear the blast of guns
far off, that echoes from town to town.

Tutta vestita a festa
la gioventù del loco
lascia le case, e per le vie si spande;
e mira ed ê mirata, e in cor s'allegra.
Io solitario in questa
rimota parte alla campagna uscendo,
ogni diletto e gioco
indugio in altro tempo: e intanto il guardo
steso nell'aria aprica
mi fere il Sol che tra lontani monti,
dopo il giorno sereno,
cadendo si dilegua, e par che dica
che la beata gioventù vien meno.

   Tu, solingo augellin, venuto a sera
del viver che daranno a te le stelle,
certo del tuo costume
non ti dorrai; che di natura è frutto
ogni vostra vaghezza.
A me, se di vecchiezza
la detestata soglia
evitar non impetro,
quando muti questi occhi all'altrui core,
e lor fia vôto il mondo, e il dì futuro
del dì presente più noioso e tetro,
che parrà di tal voglia?
che di quest'anni miei? che di me stesso?
Ahi pentirommi, e spesso,
ma sconsolato, volgerommi indietro.

Dressed in their Sunday best,
the young people of the place
leave their houses and fill the lanes;
and look about and are looked at,
and in their hearts rejoice.
I, coming out alone in this remote
part of the countryside, leave fun
and games to other times: and
meanwhile, reaching across the
open expanse, my gaze is struck
by the Sun that, sinking between
the distant hills, after the clear day,
grows weak and seems to be saying
that blessed youth is waning.

    You, lone little bird, having
come to the evening of the life
the stars will grant you, surely you
will not regret your ways; for every
whim of yours is nature's doing.
To me, if my prayers do not
keep me from the detested
threshold of old age, when
these eyes become silent to other
hearts, and the world proves
empty to them, and the coming day
more tedious and bleaker than
the present one, what will it seem like,
such a longing? what, these years
of mine? what, my own self?
Oh, I'll be sorry, and often,
but, dejected, I will look back.

LA QUIETE DOPO LA TEMPESTA
(1829)

Passata è la tempesta:
odo augellli far festa, e la gallina,
tornata in su la via,
che ripete il suo verso. Ecco il sereno
rompe là da ponente, alla montagna;
sgombrasi la campagna,
e chiaro nella valle il fiume appare.
Ogni cor si rallegra, in ogni lato
risorge il romorio
torna il lavoro usato.
L'artigiano a mirar l'umido cielo,
con l'opra in man, cantando,
fassi in su l'uscio; a prova
vien fuor la femminetta a côr dell'acqua
della novella piova;
e l'erbaiuol rinnova
di sentiero in sentiero
il grido giornaliero.
Ecco il Sol che ritorna, ecco sorride
per li poggi e le ville. Apre i balconi
apre terrazzi e logge la famiglia:
e dalla via corrente, odi lontano
tintinnio di sonagli; il carro stride
del passeggier che il suo cammin ripiglia.

   Si rallegra ogni core.
Sì dolce, sì gradita
quand' è, com'or, la vita?
quando con tanto amor
l'uomo a' suoi studi intende?
o torna all'opre? o cosa nova imprende?
quando de' mali suoi men si ricorda?

THE CALM AFTER THE STORM

The storm is over. I hear birds
rejoicing and the hen, back on
the road, takes up her refrain.
Look, the clear sky breaks there,
in the west, over the mountain;
the countryside is swept clean
and in the valley the river shows up
clearly. Every heart rejoices,
the busy hum picks up again,
familiar tasks resume.
The craftsman, singing,
his work in hand, comes to the
doorway to look up at the damp sky;
the little maid ventures out at
the sound of water flowing from
the recent rain; and the greens
vendor takes up his daily cry
from lane to lane.
Look, the sun is coming back; look,
it smiles along the hills and houses.
People inside open balconies,
terraces, and loggias: and from
the main thoroughfare comes
the far-off tinkling of harness
bells; the creaking coach of the
traveler that resumes its journey.

Every heart rejoices. When else
is life as sweet, as dear, as it is
right now? when does a man turn
to his studies or resume his tasks,
or start new work with so much love?
When does he least recall his troubles?

Piacer figlio d'affanno;
gioia vana, ch'è frutto
del passato timore, onde si scosse
e paventò la morte
chi la vita abborria;
onde in lungo tormento,
fredde, tacite, smorte,
sudâr le genti e palpitâr, vedendo
mossi alle nostre offese
folgori, nembi e vento.

   O natura cortese,
son questi i doni tuoi,
questi i diletti sono
che tu porgi ai mortali. Uscir di pena
è diletto fra noi.
Pene tu spargi a larga mano; il duolo
spontaneo sorge; e di piacer, quel tanto
che per mostro e miracolo talvolta
nasce d'affanno, è gran guadagno. Umana
prole cara agli eterni! assai felice
se respirar ti lice
d'alcun dolor: beata
se te d'ogni dolor morte risana.

Pleasure, child of misery;
empty joy, which is the fruit
of past fear, from which
rose death and terrified all those
who hated life; so that in their
protracted agony, cold, silent,
pale with fright, people trembled
and broke out in sweat, watching
thunderbolts, clouds and winds
hurled against our sins.

Oh, gracious nature, these are
your gifts, these the joys you offer
mortals. To be free of suffering
for us is joy. Suffering you sow
with lavish hand; grief springs up
of its own accord, and as for pleasure,
that bit that by some miracle or
freak of chance is born of anguish,
is great gain. The human race dear
to the gods! Happy enough if respite
is allowed you from some pain:
blessed, if death heals you of every pain.

COMMENTARY

Our ills turn out to be necessary for happiness and take on the true and real essence of good things, in the general order of nature . . . . And so we come to recognize in the violence of the elements and in other things that cause uneasiness and seem to threaten misfortune among men, both in their natural state and as members of society, as among animals too, in sickness and hundreds of other ills that plague the living, those things that prepare for and in a sense are necessary to the happiness of human beings . . . . And not just because ills underscore good things, or because we appreciate health much more after being sick, or the calm that follows a storm, but because without ills, the good things would hardly be good, since after a time they would annoy us, would lose their attraction, would no longer give us pleasure; because the sensation of pleasure, if it is really pleasing, never lasts very long.

(Pensieri IV, 8/7/1822)

Pleasure is nothing more than the abandonment and erasing of life, a kind of sleep or death. Pleasure is, more properly, the loss or decrease of feeling in us — and not a feeling in itself, least of all a lively feeling . . . . It has no positive characteristics, since it is only the lack or simply the weakening of sorrow, which is its opposite.

(Pensieri VI, 4/19/1824)

Birds are, by nature, the most contented creatures on earth . . . . Every joy and pleasant thing makes them sing; and as their joy and contentment grow, they spend more energy and breath singing. And since they sing most of the time, we assume that they are for the most part happy and cheerful! . . . . They sing more during a clear, sunny day than when it is dark and windy, and when there is a storm, or some other thing frightens them, they are silent. But once the storm is over, they begin to sing again and play with one another.

(Operetti morali, "Elogio degli uccelli," 1824)

THE HILL DESCRIBED IN "THE INFINITE"

IL SABATO DEL VILLAGGIO
(1829)

La donzelletta vien dalla campagna,
in sul calar del sole,
col suo fascio dell'erba; e reca in mano
un mazzolin di rose e di viole,
onde, siccome suole,
ornare ella si appresta
dimani, al dì di festa, il petto e il crine.
Siede con le vicine
su la scala a filar la vecchiarella,
incontro là dove si perde il giorno;
e novellando vien del suo buon tempo,
quando ai dì della festa ella si ornava,
ed ancor sana e snella
solea danzar la sera intra di quei
ch'ebbe compagni dell'età più bella.
Già tutta l'aria imbruna,
torna azzurro il sereno, e tornan l'ombre
giù da' colli e da' tetti,
al biancheggiar della recente luna.
Or la squilla dà segno
della festa che viene;
ed a quel suon diresti
che il cor si riconforta.
I fanciulli gridando
su la piazzuola in frotta,
e qua e là saltando,
fanno un lieto romore:
e intanto riede alla sua parca mensa,
fischiando, il zappatore,
e seco pensa al dì del suo riposo.

Poi, quando intorno è spenta ogni altra face,

SATURDAY IN THE VILLAGE

The little maid comes in from
the fields, as the sun goes down,
with her sheaf of grass; and carries
in her hand a tiny bunch of violets
and roses, with which tomorrow, as is
the custom on the holiday, she will
adorn her hair and breast.
The old woman sits with her
neighbors, spinning, turned
to where the day is ending;
and on she goes with stories
of old times, when she too
would adorn herself on holidays,
and, still trim and healthy,
would in the evening dance
with those who were the
friends of her best years.
Already the air darkens all around,
the limpid sky deepens to blue,
and shadows move down from
the hills and roofs with the
brightening of the rising moon.
Now bells signal the coming
holiday; and at that sound you'd say
the heart finds comfort.
Children in swarms, shouting
on the tiny square, jumping all over,
make a pleasing racket: and
meanwhile, the ploughman goes
to his meager supper, whistling,
and thinks about his day of rest.

Then when every other light is out

e tutto l'altro tace,
odi il martel picchiare, odi la sega
del legnaiuol, che veglia
nella chiusa bottega alla lucerna,
e s'affretta, e s'adopra
di fornir l'opra anzi il chiarir dell'alba.

Questo di sette è il più gradito giorno,
pien di speme e di gioia:
diman tristezza e noia
recheran l'ore, ed al travaglio usato
ciascuno in suo pensier farà ritorno.

Garzoncello scherzoso,
cotesta età fiorita
è come un giorno d'allegrezza pieno,
giorno chiaro, sereno,
che precorre alla festa di tua vita.
Godi, fanciullo mio; stato soave,
stagion lieta è cotesta.
Altro dirti non vo'; ma la tua festa
ch'anco tardi a venir non ti sia grave.

and all else around is quiet,
you hear the hammer pound,
you hear the saw of the carpenter,
who is still up by lantern light
inside his shuttered shop,
and hurries and works feverishly
to make sure the job is ready
at the crack of dawn.

This, of the seven, is the most
welcome day, full of hope and joy:
tomorrow the hours will bring sadness
and boredom, and everyone will start
thinking again about routine chores.

Mischievous boy, this flowering
age is like a day brimming with joy,
a clear day, calm, that ushers in
the holiday of your life.
Enjoy it, my boy; this is a gentle
time, a happy season.
I won't say more; but don't be
impatient if your holiday is late in coming.

COMMENTARY

Human pleasure . . . is always in the future, it is
nothing if not in the future, it exists only in the future.
Pleasure in itself cannot be grasped. I look forward to
something pleasant and I call that hope, in most cases,
pleasure. I've known pleasure; I've had a delightful expe-
rience. But all this is pleasant only because it gives us some
idea about the future, some reason to expect something
enjoyable on a large scale; it opens up a whole new circle of
hopes, convinces us we can enjoy ourselves, points out the way
to satisfy certain desires, places us in a better position with
regard to the future, both the fact and reality of it, with regard

to our own opinion and conviction, our accomplishments, the improvements we anticipate as a result of experience. . . .

So: I feel pleasure. In what way exactly? Each instant in the action we call pleasure is relative with respect to each successive instant; and it is not pleasant except in relation to the moments that follow, that is to say, to the future. The pleasure I experience in this very instant is not enough, and since it does not satisfy me it is not fully pleasure. But surely I *will* know it in this very next moment, surely my pleasure will increase and I shall be fully satisfied. Let's take it further: I still haven't experienced real pleasure, but I will any moment now (who can doubt it?). Such is the reasoning, the concern, the operation, the way, the emotion of the soul in the very moment of pleasure, of any kind of pleasant sensation. When the last moment is reached and pleasure has come to an end, man still has not grasped it; he may feel frustrated or content, it doesn't matter, because both are the result of a false notion, a weak and hardly convincing prejudice that he has indeed grasped it. And he goes on thinking about it, recalling what he felt and in doing that he experiences another pleasure, the object of which is in the past, to be sure, but not the pleasure itself (for how can something be in the past when it has never actually been and is always a thing in the future?), and the experience of this new pleasure turns out to be a series of moments of the same kind as the others, and therefore equally in the future . . . . Pleasure therefore is never either in the past or in the present, but always and solely in the future. And the reason is that for a human being true pleasure can be nothing else but infinite (infinite in each of its moments and actually so); and it can never be infinite, even though we all entertain a dim notion that it can be or will be, or that even if it isn't exactly infinite it is nonetheless pleasant. And this belief (natural and essential to man and inspired by nature) is what is commonly called pleasure and is all that can be expected of pleasure. Therefore the only pleasure that exists is a future pleasure . . . .

(Pensieri II, 1/20/21)

At this very moment I know pleasure, I would like these same circumstances, just as they are at this moment, to continue for the rest of my life, for all eternity. No man can say this or say it in good faith, not even for a single instant, not even in the midst of the greatest pleasure possible. For, if in that moment his pleasure were truly present and perfect (if not perfect, it cannot be pleasure) naturally he will want it to continue forever, since the end of man is pleasure; he would therefore want his entire life to be what it is in that moment, more than that even: to live forever so that he can have pleasure forever. But the simple truth is that no man has ever formulated or entertained such a wish, not even in the happiest moments of his life or while actually experiencing those moments. The simple truth is even the man, whoever he may be, who has enjoyed or is about to enjoy the greatest human pleasure possible cannot, will never entertain that thought for a single moment. Because even at that moment of greatest pleasure, no one is ever completely satisfied or has ever abandoned in any way the desire and the hope for a still greater and greater pleasure. So that his pleasure could not have been true and present, at that moment, although, once it is past, we wish that our entire life could have been like that and express that wish to ourselves and others as though we meant it. It's wrong, of course; for if ever we should attain that end, we would stop praising it.

(Pensieri V, 7/3/23)

CANTO NOTTURNO DI UN PASTORE ERRANTE DELL'ASIA
(1829-1830)

Che fai tu, luna, in ciel? dimmi, che fai,
silenziosa luna?
Sorgi la sera, e vai,
contemplando i deserti; indi ti posi.
Ancor non sei tu paga
di riandare i sempiterni calli?
ancor non prendi a schivo, ancor sei vaga
di mirar queste valli?
Somiglia alla tua vita
la vita del pastore.
Sorge in sul primo albore,
move la greggia oltre pel campo, e vede
greggi, fontane ed erbe;
poi stanco si riposa in su la sera:
altro mai non ispera.
Dimmi, o luna: a che vale
al pastor la sua vita,
la vostra vita a voi? dimmi: ove tende
questo vagar mio breve,
il tuo corso immortale?

   Vecchierel bianco, infermo,
mezzo vestito e scalzo,
con gravissimo fascio in su le spalle,
per montagna e per valle,
per sassi acuti, ed alta rena, e fratte,
al vento, alla tempesta, e quando avvampa
l'ora, e quando poi gela,
corre via, corre, anela,

NIGHT SONG OF A
WANDERING SHEPHERD
OF ASIA

What do you do, moon, there
in the sky? tell me, silent moon,
what do you do? You rise in the
evening and keep moving,
contemplating deserts; then you set.
Haven't you had your fill yet
of tracking those everlasting paths?
Are you not weary yet of these
valleys, are you still pleased to see them?
Your life is like the shepherd's life.
He's up at the first glimmer of light,
moves his flock further out in the field,
and sees springs, flocks, and grasses;
then tired, he rests as evening falls:
never longs for anything more.
Tell me, moon: what good is the
shepherd's life to him? your life to you?
tell me, where is my brief wandering,
your immortal course, heading?

White-haired, weak old man,
unshod, half-clothed,
a crushing sheaf upon his back,
rushes over mountain and valley,
over sharp rocks and deep sands
and thickets, into the wind, into
the storm, and when it's blistering
hot and then when it's freezing,
rushes on, breathless, crosses torrents
and swamps, falls, gets up,

103

cade, risorge, e più e più s'affretta,
senza posa o ristoro,
lacero, sanguinoso; infin ch'arriva
colà dove la via
e dove il tanto affaticar fu vòlto:
abisso orrido, immenso,
ov'ei precipitando, il tutto obblia.
Vergine luna, tale
è la vita mortale.

   Nasce l'uomo a fatica,
ed è rischio di morte il nascimento.
Prova pena e tormento
per prima cosa; e in sul principio stesso
la madre e il genitore
il prende a consolar dell'esser nato.
Poi che crescendo viene,
l'uno e l'altro il sostiene, e via pur sempre
con atti e con parole
studiosi fargli core,
e consolarlo dell'umano stato:
altro ufficio più grato
non si fa da parenti alla lor prole.
Ma perché dare al sole,
perché reggere in vita
che poi di quella consolar convenga?
Se la vita è sventura,
perché da noi si dura?
Intatta luna, tale
è lo stato mortale.
Ma tu mortal non sei,
e forse del mio dir poco ti cale.

   Pur tu, solinga, eterna peregrina,
che sì pensosa sei, tu forse intendi,
questo viver terreno,

and hurries more and more,
without stop or rest,
scarred and bleeding;
until he comes to where his course
and so much effort were directed:
a horrible immense abyss, plunging
into which he blots out everything.
Chaste moon, such
is this mortal life.

   Man is born with great labor,
and birth is risk of death.
The first things he feels
are pain and misery; and from
the very start, mother and father
take to soothing him for having
being born. Then, as he grows
older, one and the other
encourage him, and go on trying
their best, always, with words
and actions, to give him
strength and comfort him
for his human state:
no more welcome service
can parents offer their children.
But why bring to light, why nurture
life in one who then must be
consoled for it? If life is misfortune,
why do we endure it? Untainted moon,
such is our mortal state. But you
are not mortal, and my words may
matter little if anything to you.

   Yet you, lonely, eternal wanderer,
you who who are so thoughtful, you
maybe understand this earthly life,

il patir nostro, il sospirar, che sia;
che sia questo morir, questo supremo
scolorar del sembiante,
e perir dalla terra, e venir meno
ad ogni usata, amante compagnia.
E tu certo comprendi
il perché delle cose, e vedi il frutto
del mattin, della sera,
del tacito, infinito andar del tempo.
Tu sai, tu certo, a qual suo dolce amore
rida la primavera,
a chi giovi l'ardore, e che procacci
il verno co' suoi ghiacci.
Mille cose sai tu, mille discopri,
che son celate al semplice pastore.
Spesso quand'io ti miro
star così muta in sul deserto piano,
che, in suo giro lontano, al ciel confina;
ovver con la mia greggia
seguirmi viaggiando a mano a mano;
e quando miro in cielo arder le stelle;
dico fra me pensando:
a che tante facelle?
che fa l'aria infinita, e quel profondo
infinito seren? che vuol dir questa
solitudine immensa? ed io che sono?
Così meco ragiono: e della stanza
smisurata e superba,
e dell'innumerabile famiglia;
poi di tanto adoprar, di tanti moti
d'ogni celeste, ogni terrena cosa,
girando senza posa,
per tornar sempre là donde son mosse;
uso alcuno, alcun frutto
indovinar non so. Ma tu per certo,
giovinetta immortal, conosci il tutto.

what our suffering, our tears
are all about; what our dying means,
this final draining of color from the face,
and to leave earth, and lose all our
beloved long-time friends. And you, surely,
grasp the why of things, you see the fruit
of morning, of evening, of the silent,
infinite passing of time.
You know, surely you must, to what
sweet love Spring smiles, who profits
from summer's heat, and what is
gained from winter with its ice.
Thousands of things you know,
thousands you uncover that are
hidden from a poor shepherd.
Often when I watch you keep
so still above the open plain,
which in its farthest curve touches
the sky; or else follow me and my flock
step by step along the way: and when
I gaze up at the stars shining in the sky;
I ask myself: what for, so many lights?
what is that infinite expanse doing there,
and that deep, infinite calm?
what does it mean, this vast
solitude? and what am I?
Such are my thoughts: and about
awesome immeasurable space, and the
countless beings it holds; then about
so much striving, so much movement
of every celestial, every terrestrial thing,
all turning without rest,
to come back, always, where they first
began; to what purpose, to what end
I cannot guess. But you, surely,
you know everything, immortal maid.

Questo io conosco e sento,
che degli eterni giri,
che dell'esser mio frale,
qualche bene o contento
avrà fors'altro; a me la vita è male.

   O greggia mia che posi, oh te beata,
che la miseria tua, credo, non sai!
Quanta invidia ti porto!
Non sol perchè d'affanno
quasi libera vai;
ch'ogni stento, ogni danno,
ogni estremo timor subito scordi;
ma più perchè giammai tedio non provi.
Quando tu siedi all'ombra, sovra l'erbe,
tu se' queta e contenta;
e gran parte dell'anno
senza noia consumi in quello stato.
Ed io pur seggo sovra l'erba, all'ombra,
e un fastidio m'ingombra
la mente, ed uno spron quasi mi punge
sì che, sedendo, più che mai son lunge
da trovar pace or loco.
E pur nulla non bramo,
e non ho fino a qui cagion di pianto.
Quel che tu goda o quanto,
non so già dir; ma fortunata sei.
Ed io godo ancor poco,
o greggia mia, né di ciò sol mi lagno.
Se tu parlar sapessi, io chiederei:
dimmi: perché giacendo
a bell'agio, ozioso,
s'appaga ogni animale;
me, s'io giaccio in riposo, il tedio assale?

   Forse s'avess'io l'ale

108

This much I know and feel: that from
these endless turns, that from my fragile
being, another may derive some good
or satisfaction: life, for me, is bad.

Oh, flock of mine that rest here,
oh, you are blessed, I'm sure, for
you know nothing of your plight!
How much I envy you!
Not only because you're free, almost,
of suffering; for, whatever burden,
whatever injury befalls you,
even the worst fear, you quickly
forget, but, even more, because
you will never know tedium.
When you sit in the shade, on the grass,
you are calm and content;
and you spend the greater part
of the year that way, without boredom.
And I too sit on the grass, in the shade,
and a worry crowds my mind, an urge
almost pierces me, so that sitting here,
I am further than ever from finding
peace or rest. And yet I long for
nothing, and have had all this while
no reason for tears.
What you find joy in, or how much,
I have no way of telling; but you are
fortunate. And I, dear flock of mine,
I still have little joy, nor do I complain
only of that. If you could speak, I'd ask:
why is it that every animal is content
to lie at ease, do nothing; me, if I lie
down to rest, tedium crushes?

Maybe if I had wings to fly above

da volar su le nubi,
e noverar le stelle ad una ad una,
o come il tuono errar di giogo in giogo,
più felice sarei, dolce mia greggia,
più felice sarei, candida luna.
O forse erra dal vero,
mirando all'altrui sorte, il mio pensiero:
forse in qual forma, in quale
stato che sia, dentro covile o cuna,
è funesto a chi nasce il dì natale.

the clouds and one by one count off
the stars, or like thunder,
roam from peak to peak,
I would be happier, sweet flock of mine,
I would be happier, pale moon.
Or maybe, my thoughts stray
from the truth, wondering sbout
the fate of others: maybe, in whatever
form, whatever state, in sheepfold
or in cradle, for anyone who's born
ill-fated is the day of birth.

COMMENTARY

The very birth of man, that is, the beginning of his life
is a great threat to his life. Witness how many die at birth
unable to withstand the difficulties and dangers of coming
into the world. Mind you, I think if one examines the matter
he will find that among beasts the number that die at birth is
in proportion much lower, no doubt because human nature
in its civilizing process grew weak and rotten.

(Pensieri, I, 1819)

As soon as a child is born, at that very moment that
his mother gives birth to him, she must comfort him, soothe
his crying, lessen the burden of the existence which she has
given him. And one of the chief responsibilities of good
parents, when the child is growing up, is to encourage him in
life, comfort him, because pain and ills and passions are
heaviest in that period of life, much more so than for those
whose long experience has given them an advantage or who
simply by virtue of having lived longer have learned to bear
them. A good father and mother must . . . reassure their
children, . . . make tolerable the mistake they made in giving
birth to them. Good God! Why is man born in the first place?
And why does he give birth? To reassure those he has
brought into the world for having beeen born?

(Pensieri, IV, 5/13/1822)

Who in his right mind can ever look upon the awesome miraculous work of nature, the vast though artificial complex of the planets, and call it a void nothing? although the truth is it can serve us in no way at all, can never lead to happiness, which must always be the end and perfection of human life, in fact the only useful thing that life has to offer.

(Pensieri, V, 7/10/1823)

Life? It's the journey of a sick and crippled man who carries a tremendous burden on his back and works his way up and down mountains, through dangerous and difficult places, through snow and sleet and rain and wind and unbearable heat, on and on, never once resting, until at last after many long days he comes to the edge of an abyss or a deep ditch and falls headlong into it.

(Pensieri, VII, 1/17/1826)

Everything is rotten. That is, everything that is, is rotten; that anybody should exist at all, is rotten; everything exists for a rotten end; existence is a rotten thing and its end is rotten; the end of the universe is rotten; the state, order, laws, the natural motions of the universe are all rotten, and their ultimate purpose nothing but rotten. There is no other good but that of not being alive; . . . . . Although this kind of thinking may shock our sensibilities, that will not have it that the end of things is anything but good, it may turn out to be more solid than that of Leibnitz, etc., for whom everything is good. But then I would never presume to extend this thought to the point of saying that this universe is the worst of all possible universes. Who knows the limits of the possible?

(Pensieri, VII, 4/22/1826)

AERIAL VIEW OF THE MARCHE COUNTRYSIDE

113

AMORE E MORTE
(1832)

Fratelli, a un tempo stesso, Amor e Morte
ingenerò la sorte.
Cose quaggiù sì belle
altre il mondo non ha, non han le stelle.
Nasce dall'uno il bene,
nasce il piacer maggiore
che per lo mar dell'essere si trova;
l'altra ogni gran dolore,
ogni gran male annulla.
Bellissima fanciulla,
dolce a veder, non quale
la si dipinge la codarda gente,
gode il fanciullo Amore
accompagnar sovente;
e sorvolano insiem la via mortale,
primi conforti d'ogni saggio core.
Né cor fu mai più saggio
che percosso d'amor, né mai più forte
sprezzò l'infausta vita,
né per altro signore
come per questo a perigliar fu pronto:
ch'ove tu porgi aita,
Amor, nasce il coraggio,
e si ridesta; e sapiente in opre,
non in pensier invan, siccome suole,
divien l'umana prole.

Quando novellamente
nasce nel cor profondo
un amoroso affetto,
languido e stanco insieme con esso in petto
un desiderio di morir si sente:

114

LOVE AND DEATH

Fate conceived, at one time,
siblings, Love and Death.
The earth down here has no
other things so beautiful,
nor have the stars.
Born of the first is goodness,
born is the greatest pleasure
found in the whole sea
of being; the other eliminates
every great suffering, every
great ill. A most beautiful
maid, sweet to behold,
not as the cowardly paint her,
she very often gladly goes forth
with the boy, Love, and together
they hover above our mortal
path, foremost comfort
of every wise heart.
Nor was heart ever wiser
than when struck by love, nor
did it ever more resolutely
scorn this hapless life, nor
was it ever more ready to face
dangers for any other but
this master: where you offer help,
Love, courage is born and
reawakens; and the human race
grows wise in deeds, not idle
speculation, as so often is the case.

   When first a loving impulse
is born deep in the heart,
together with it, a listless and weary
yearning to die fills the breast:

come non so: ma tale
d'amor vero e possente è il primo effetto.
Forse gli occhi spaura
allor questo deserto: a sé la terra
forse il mortale inabitabil fatta
vede omai senza quella
nova, sola, infinita
felicità che il suo pensier figura:
ma per cagion di lei grave procella
presentendo in suo cor, brama quiete,
brama raccôrsi in porto
dinanzi al fier disio,
che già, rugghiando, intorno intorno oscura.

   Poi, quando tutto avvolge
la formidabil possa,
e fulmina nel cor l'invitta cura,
quante volte implorata
con desidero intenso,
Morte, sei tu dall'affannono amante!
Quante la sera, e quante
abbandonando all'alba il corpo stanco,
sé beato chiamò s'indi giammai
non rilevasse il fianco,
né tornasse a veder l'amara luce!
E spesso al suon della funebre squilla,
al canto che conduce
la gente morta al sempiterno obblio,
con più sospiri ardenti
dall'imo petto invidiò colui
che tra gli spenti ad abitar sen giva.
Fin la negletta plebe,
l'uom della villa, ignaro
d'ogni virtù che da saper deriva,
fin la donzella timidetta e schiva,
che già di morte al nome

how, I don't know: but such
is the immediate reaction to a true
and mighty love. It may be that this
desert frightens the eyes, then:
it may be that man then sees
the earth made uninhabitable for him
without that one new infinite joy
pictured in his mind: but fearing
in his heart a great storm brewing
because of it, he craves quiet,
craves safe harbor against the fierce
desire that already rumbling,
moves closer, closer, darkening.

   Then when the awesome force
has overwhelmed all things,
and unconquered passion strikes
the heart, how many times
are you invoked, Death, with most
intense desire by the tormented lover!
How many, at night, and yielding up
the weary body at dawn, how many
times he counted himself blessed
if only he were never to rise
from there again, never again set eyes
on the harsh light of day!
And often at the sound of tolling
bells, of dirges that bear those gone,
into endless oblivion, with the most
anguished sighs from deep inside his breast,
he envied him who was about to make
his home among the dead.
Even the lowest of us, the peasant,
ignorant of every virtue that comes
from knowledge, even the shy and
timid little maid who at the first mention

sentì rizzar le chiome,
osa a la tomba, alle funeree bende
fermar lo sgardo di costanza pieno,
osa ferro e veleno
meditar lungamente,
e nell'indotta mente
la gentilezza del morir comprende.
Tanto alla morte inclina
d'amor la disciplina. Anco sovente,
a tal venuto il gran travaglio interno
che sostener nol può forza mortale,
o cede il corpo frale
ai terribili moti, e in questa forma
pel fraterno poter Morte prevale;
o così sprona Amor là nel profondo,
che da se stessi il villanello ignaro,
la tenera donzella
con la man violenta
pongon le membra giovanili in terra.
Ride ai lor casi il mondo,
a cui pace e vecchiezza il ciel consenta.

 Ai fervidi, ai felici,
agli animosi ingegni
l'uno o l'altro di voi conceda il fato,
dolci signori, amici
all'umana famiglia,
al cui poter nessun poter somiglia
nell'immenso universo, e non l'avanza,
se non quella del fato, altra possanza.
E tu, cui già dal cominciar degli anni
sempre onorata invoco,
bella Morte, pietosa
tu sola al mondo dei terreni affanni,
se celebrata mai
fosti da me, s'al tuo divino stato

of the word death would feel her hair
stand up, can fix her unwavering gaze
upon the grave, upon funereal
trappings, can brood at length
about sharp steel and poison,
and grasps in her untutored mind
the ease of dying. This far the training
of love will favor death. Often, also,
when the great suffering inside has
reached that point where human
strength can't bear it any longer,
either the frail body yields under
the terrible strain, and in this manner,
through brotherly power,
Death prevails; or else Love prods
in such a way from deep within,
that all by themselves, the simple
peasant lad, the tender maid
with their own violent hands consign
their young bodies to the earth.
The world laughs at their plight, to whom
may heaven bring peace and old age.

    To the zealous, the happy, the talented
spirits among you, may fate grant, one
or another, kind masters, friends
of the human family, whose power
no other power in the vast universe
resembles, nor any other surpasses,
except that of fate.
And you I entreat, fair Death, who
from my earliest years I've always
honored, you alone in the world
with pity for our earthly trials,
if ever praised by me, if ever I strove
to make amends for all the insults

l'onte del volgo ingrato
ricompensar tentai,
non tardar più, t'inchina
a disusati preghi,
chiudi alla luce omai
questi occhi tristi, o dell'età reina.
Me certo troverai, qual si sia l'ora
che tu le penne al mio pregar dispieghi,
erta la fronte, armato,
e renitente al fato,
la man che flaggellando si colora
nel mio sangue innocente
non ricolmar di lode,
non benedir, com'usa
per antica viltà l'umana gente;
ogni vana speranza onde consola
sé coi fanciulli il mondo,
ogni conforto stolto
gittar da me; null'altro in alcun tempo
sperar, se non te sola;
solo aspettar sereno
quel dì ch'io pieghi addormentato il volto
nel tuo virgineo seno.

of the ungrateful rabble to your
divine being, delay no more,
bend to these uncommon prayers,
close these sad eyes to the light,
at last, oh queen of ages.
Me, for certain, you will find,
at whatever hour you unfold
your wings in answer to my prayers,
head high, armed and resolute
against fate, not blessing,
not heaping praise, as people
have been doing from ancient
cowardice, on the hand that,
flogging, turns red with my
innocent blood; flinging from me
every foolish comfort, every vain
hope by which the world consoles
itself as with children;
hoping for nothing else, ever,
except you only; waiting alone,
serene, for that day when
in sleep I lower my face
upon your virgin breast.

COMMENTARY

Even as a child I craved glory and fame. It was obvious
in all that I did — in the games I played . . . . the re-enactment
of Homeric battles in our garden, where we used rocks . . . .
sticks . . . etc. . . . assuming Homeric names, or rather those
recorded in books about Roman history, particularly the civil
wars — in which I was most interested — insisting that I be
called Scipio . . . . reciting my Latin speech against Caesar to
my father, putting down my hatred for the tyrant and my
enthusiastic joy when I read about his assassination. We used
to carry on like this about everything we read: I always chose

to be Pompey . . . and would force [my brother] Charles to play Caesar, which he did with extreme dislike.

(Scritti vari, 1817)

Many times, when the burdens of body and soul grew oppressive, I yearned not just for rest; my whole being indulged quite naturally, without any effort or heroics, the possibility of an unconscious state without limits, eternal; a state of rest that was continuous inaction of soul and body. My reason identified that end, which my whole being craved so much at those moments, as Death — but it did not frighten me at all. Many sick people, who are not heroes, nor courageous, who are quite fearful in fact, have yearned for and at this very moment yearn for death, in the midst of great pain, and the thought of it brings a kind of peace . . . . In my case, the thing I wanted and that I found especially attractive was a kind of rest that was eternal, from which I would never wake again or have to pick up again the same burdens that had worn me out.

(Pensieri I, 10/21/1820)

Men are weaklings and cowards, their souls are narrow and petty; always ready to hope for the best, since they are perfectly willing to change the meaning of what is good depending on the circumstances of their lives; quick — as Petrarch says — to surrender their arms to fortune; resigned completely to every and all misfortune, ready to compromise in any way at all for what has been denied them or what they have lost; amenable to any conditions, to the most barbarous and demeaning fate — and when every other hope is gone, capable of believing lies . . . . For my part, I — like the people of the Mediterranean, who laugh at husbands who are in love with their unfaithful wives — laugh at mankind thus in love with life. To let oneself be deluded and betrayed like idiots is not civilized in my judgment; one is not only burdened with sorrows, he becomes a kind of joke, the butt of nature and fate. I am not speaking of the illusions of the imagination but of the mind. Maybe these feelings are the result of some illness, I don't know; all I know is that sick or well I detest the cowardice of men, I will not accept any childish illusion or relief; and I have enough courage to live with the loss of hope, to examine unflinchingly the desert of my life without lying about the reality of human misery, to accept the consequences of a very painful but very true philosophy. And if it works for us in no other way, at least it provides strong men with the bold satisfaction of seeing every veil stripped from the mysterious and hidden cruelty of human destiny.

(Operette morali, Dialogo di Tristano e di un Amico)

The moment of death is anything but painful or uncomfortable, or excruciating; the bodily ills that occasion it no matter how serious (in fact, the more serious they are, the truer this is), cease altogether as death approaches; and the moment of death itself, and those preceding it, are moments of absolute rest and relief, matching in their intensity the pain and suffering that led to that point. What I have said about the struggle of the body applies also to that of the spirit, for when the patient has reached that point of unconsciousness where he is oblivious to all bodily pain, even though the conditions that produced it are still there and still serious, as invariably happens at the moment of death, the soul — almost outside of the senses — is quite beside itself, beyond spiritual awareness (which operates only through the bodily senses) and is therefore unable to feel the pain and the struggle of the mind. In fact, the moment of death is always preceded by the loss of speech, total unconsciousness, an incapacity to grasp or formulate anything, as is clear from all the external signs and is certainly the case when one sleeps or faints.

(Pensieri, IV, 11/28/1821)

A SE STESSO
(1833)

Or poserai per sempre,
stanco mio cor. Perì l'inganno estremo,
ch'eterno io mi credei. Perì. Ben sento,
in noi di cari inganni,
non che la speme, il desiderio è spento.
Posa per sempre. Assai
palpitasti. Non val cosa nessuna
i moti tuoi, né di sospiri é degna
la terra. Amaro e noia
la vita, altro mai nulla; e fango é il mondo.
T'acqueta omai. Dispera
l'ultima volta. Al gener nostro il fato
non donò che il morire. Omai disprezza
te, la natura, il brutto
poter che, ascoso, a comun danno impera,
e l'infinita vanità del tutto.

TO HIMSELF

Now you will rest forever,
my weary heart. The last illusion,
I thought eternal, died. Well I know
that not only hope but the yearning
for cherished illusions is spent in me.
Rest forever. Much you endured.
They count for nothing,
your feelings, nor is the earth
worth tears. Tedium and bitterness,
life, never anything else;
and the world is slime.
Calm yourself, now. Despair for the
last time. Fate granted our race
nothing but dying. Spurn finally
yourself, nature, the ugly power
that, hidden, lords it over
our common woes,
and the infinite vanity of things.

ASPASIA
(1834)

Torna dinanzi al mio pensier talora
il tuo sembiante, Aspasia. O fuggitivo
per abitati lochi a me lampeggia
in altri volti; o per deserti campi,
al dì sereno, alle tacenti stelle,
da soave armonia quasi ridesta,
nell'alma a sgomentarsi ancor vicina
quella superba vision risorge.
Quando adorata, o numi, e quale un giorno
mia delizia ed erinni! E mai non sento
mover profumo di fiorita piaggia,
né di fiori olezzar vie cittadine,
ch'io non ti vegga ancor qual eri il giorno
che ne' vezzosi appartamenti accolta,
tutti odorati dei novelli fiori
di primavera, del color vestita
della bruna viola, a me si offerse
l'angelica tua forma, inchino il fianco
sovra nitide pelli, e circonfusa
d'arcana voluttà; quando tu, dotta
allettatrice, fervidi sonanti
baci scoccavi nelle curve labbra
de' tuoi bambini, il nievo collo intanto
porgendo, e lor di tue cagioni ignari
con la man leggiadrissima stringevi
al seno ascoso e desiato. Apparve
novo ciel, nova terra, e quasi un raggio
divino al pensier mio. Così nel fianco
non punto inerme a viva forza impresse
il tuo braccio lo stral, che poscia fitto
ululando portai finch'a quel giorno
si fu due volte ricondotto il sole.

ASPASIA

Your face rises before me again, from
time to time, Aspasia. It flashes, fleeting,
among crowded places, in other faces;
or in deserted fields on a clear day, under
silent stars, almost as though awakened
by soft harmony, that glorious vision rises
again, still close, to spread panic in my soul.
How much adored, oh gods, how once
my pleasure and despair! And I can never
feel the waft of perfume from a flowering
garden, or flowers filling the city streets
with their odors, without still seeing you
as you were that day, when in the privacy
of your attractive rooms, filled with the
scent of fresh Spring flowers, clad in
the color of dark violet, reclining to
one side on the soft furs, and
circumfused with dark desire, your
angelic form displayed itself to me;
when, most accomplished temptress,
you pressed fervent resounding kisses
on the pursed lips of your children,
while arching your snow-white neck,
and with the most delicate gesture
drew them close, who did not know
your real intent, crowding them
to your veiled and most desired breast.
A new heaven, a new earth opened up
for me, a light almost divine. And so,
with your sure arm you drove the arrow
deep into my side, and though not
unprepared, I carried it buried inside
me, all the while howling, until the sun
twice came around full circle to that day.

Raggio divino al mio pensier apparve,
donna, la tua beltà. Simile effetto
fan la bellezza e i musicali accordi,
ch'alto mistero d'ignorati Elisi
paion sovente rivelar. Vagheggia
il piagato mortal quindi la figlia
della sua mente, l'amorosa idea,
che gran parte d'Olimpo in sé racchiude,
tutta al volto ai costumi alla favella
pari alla donna che il rapito amante
vagheggiare ed amar confuso estima.
Or questa egli non già, ma quella, ancora
nei corporali amplessi, inchina ed ama.
Alfin l'errore e gli scambiati oggetti
conoscendo, s'adira; e spesso incolpa
la donna a torto. A quella eccelsa imago
sorge di rado il femminile ingegno;
e ciò che inspira ai generosi amanti
la sua stessa beltà, donna non pensa,
né comprender potria. Non cape in quelle
anguste fronti ugual concetto. E male
al vivo sfolgorar di quegli sguardi
spera l'uomo ingannato, e mal richiede
sensi profondi, sconosciuti, e molto
più che virili, in chi dell'uomo al tutto
da natura è minor. Che se più molli
e più tenui le membra, essa la mente
men capace e men forte anco riceve.

Né tu finor giammai quel che tu stessa
inspirasti alcun tempo al mio pensiero
potesti, Aspasia, immaginar. Non sai
che smisurato amor, che affanni intensi,
che indicibili moti e che deliri
movesti in me; né verrà tempo alcuno
che tu l'intenda. In simil guisa ignora

Your loveliness, my lady, appeared
to my mind divine radiance. A similar
effect have beauty and musical harmonies,
which often seem to unfold deep mysteries
of unknown Edens. And so, the stricken
mortal admires the child of his imagination,
love's ideal image, which carries within it
a large part of Olympus, similar in face,
manner, speech, to the woman whom,
having confused the ideal with the real.
the smitten lover favors. Not this one,
but the other, he now worships and adores,
even when making love. Finally, realizing
his error in having mistaken one thing
for another, he grows angry; and often
wrongly blames the woman. Female intellect
rarely rises to that exalted image; and what
her own beauty inspires in her generous lovers,
a woman cannot imagine or understand.
Such a thought won't fit inside that elegant
brow. And thus misled, man hopes in vain
at the bright flashing of those glances, and
is wrong to expect unknown, deep sensibilities,
much more than virile, in one who is by nature,
in every way, inferior to man. For if softer
and more delicate her limbs, she also
receives a mind less capable, less strong.

What you yourself inspired in my
thoughts for a time, you could not,
to this day, ever have imagined, Aspasia.
You don't know what inordinate passion,
what fierce pangs, what inexpressible
feelings and wild fantasies you roused
in me; nor will there ever come a time
when you will understand. In like manner,

129

esecutor di musici concenti
quel ch'ei con mano o con la voce adopra
in chi l'ascolta. Or quell'Aspasia è morta
che tanto amai. Giace per sempre, oggetto
della mia vita un dì: se non se quanto,
pur come cara larva, ad ora ad ora
tornar costuma e disparir. Tu vivi,
bella non solo ancor, ma bella tanto,
al parer mio, che tutte l'altre avanzi.
Pur quell'ardor che da te nacque è spento:
perch'io te non amai, ma quella Diva
che già vita, or sepolcro, ha nel mio core.
Quella adorai gran tempo; e sì mi piacque
sua celeste beltà, ch'io, per insino
già dal principio conoscente e chiaro
dell'esser tuo, dell'arti e delle frodi,
pur ne' tuoi contemplando i suoi begli occhi,
cupido ti seguii finch'ella visse,
ingannato non già, ma dal piacere
di quella dolce somiglianza un lungo
servaggio ed aspro a tollerar condotto.

   Or ti vanta, che il puoi. Narra che sola
sei del tuo sesso a cui piegar sostenni
l'altero capo, a cui spontaneo porsi
l'indomito mio cor. Narra che prima,
e spero ultima certo, il ciglio mio
supplichevol vedesti, a te dinanzi
me timido, tremante (ardo in ridirlo
di sdegno e di rossor), me di me privo,
ogni tua voglia, ogni parola, ogni atto
spiar sommessamente, a' tuoi superbi
fastidi impallidir, brillare in volto
ad un segno cortese, ad ogni sguardo
mutar forma e color. Cadde l'incanto,
e spezzato con esso, a terra sparso

one who produces musical harmonies is
unaware of the effect his hand or voice
has on those who listen. The Aspasia I once
loved so much is now dead. Buried forever,
once the sole object of my life: except for when,
like a friendly ghost, from time to time she
happens to turn up, then disappear. You live,
not just still beautiful, but, in my judgment,
so beautiful that you surpass all others.
Yet, the passion you aroused is spent: for it
wasn't you I loved but that Divinity who once
had life, now has a sepulcher in my heart.
That one I worshipped a very long time;
and her celestial beauty pleased me so, that
although aware and clear from the beginning
about your true being, of your artful and
crafty ways, even while contemplating in yours
her lovely eyes, I followed you eagerly,
so long as she lived, not in the least deceived,
but compelled by the pleasure of that sweet
likeness to endure a long and bitter servitude.

Boast now, for you can. Tell how
you are the only one among your sex
to whom I let my proud head bend,
to whom spontaneously I offered my
unconquered heart. Tell how you were
the first, and last, I hope, to see my
suppliant brow, me timid before you,
trembling (I blush with shame and anger
recalling it), me, not myself, wait humbly on
your every wish, your every word and gesture,
grow pale at your imperious complaints,
grow red in the face at some sign of
kindness, change color and aspect at every
look. The spell was broken, and, shattered
with it, the yoke scattered on the ground:

131

il giogo: onde m'allegro. E sebben pieni
di tedio, alfin dopo il servire e dopo
un lungo vaneggiar, contento abbraccio
senno con libertà. Che se d'affetti
orba la vita, e di gentili errori,
è notte senza stelle a mezzo il verno,
già del fato mortale a me bastante
e conforto e vendetta è che su l'erba
qui neghittoso immobile giacendo,
il mar la terra e il ciel miro e sorrido.

for that I rejoice. And after serving
and after dreaming so long in vain,
I finally welcome, content, both wisdom
and freedom, though full of tedium.
For if life is bereft of emotions and tender
illusions, a mid-winter's night without stars,
to me, revenge and comfort enough now
for our mortal fate is that, lying here
on the grass, idle, unmoving, I gaze
at the sea, the earth, the sky and smile.

LA GINESTRA O IL FIORE DEL DESERTO

(1836)

Qui su l'arida schiena
del formidabil monte
sterminator Vesevo,
la qual null'altro allegra arbor né fiore,
tuoi cespi solitari intorno spargi,
odorata ginestra,
contenta dei deserti. Anco ti vidi
de' tuoi steli abbelir l'erme contrade
che cingon la cittade
la qual fu donna de' mortali un tempo,
e del perduto impero
par che col grave e taciturno aspetto
faccian fede e ricordo al passeggero.
Or ti riveggo in questo suol, di tristi
lochi e dal mondo abbandonati amante,
e d'afflitte fortune ognor compagna.
Questi campi cosparsi
di ceneri infeconde, e ricoperti
dell'impietrata lava,
che sotto i passi al peregrin risona;
dove s'annida e si contorce al sole
la serpe, e dove al noto
cavernoso covil torna il coniglio;
fûr liete ville e colti,
e biondeggiâr di spiche, e risonâro
di muggito d'armenti;
fûr giardini e palagi,
agli ozi de' potenti
gradito ospizio; e fûr città famose
che coi torrenti suoi l'altero monte
dall'ignea bocca fulminando oppresse

THE BROOM, OR,
THE DESERT FLOWER

Here, on the scorched back
of the awesome mountain, Vesuvius
the destroyer, where no other tree
or flower cheers up the place,
you scatter your solitary clusters,
fragrant broom, content
with wastelands. I saw you, also,
grace with your stems the solitary
tracts that circle the city once queen
of men, and with their grave
and silent aspect seemed to bear
witness to and recall for the passer-by
the fallen empire. I see you again
now, in this soil, lover of melancholy
sites abandoned by the world,
and ever faithful companion
of afflicted fortunes. These fields
strewn with sterile ashes and covered
with hardened lava that echoes
to the visitor's footsteps, where
the snake nests and writhes in the
sun and where the rabbit turns into
his cavernous familiar warren;
were happy villas and rich fields,
and shimmered gold with corn,
and echoed with lowing of kine;
were gardens and mansions, welcome
retreats for the pastimes of the mighty;
and were famous cities which
the haughty mountain, surprising with
torrents from its fiery mouth, crushed,
together with all their inhabitants.

con gli abitanti insieme. Or tutto intorno
una ruina involve,
dove tu siedi, o fior gentile, e quasi
i danni altrui commiserando, al cielo
di dolcissimo odor mandi un profumo,
che il deserto consola. A queste piagge
venga colui che d'esaltar con lode
il nostro stato ha in uso, e vegga quanto
è il genere nostro in cura
all'amante natura. E la possanza
qui con giusta misura
anco estimar potrà dell'uman seme,
cui la dura nutrice, ov'ei men teme,
con lieve moto in un momento annulla
in parte, e può con moti
poco men lievi ancor subitamente
annichilare in tutto.
Dipinte in queste rive
son dell'umana gente
le magnifiche sorti e progressive.

Qui mira e qui ti specchia,
secol superbo e sciocco,
chi il calle insino allora
dal risorto pensier segnato innanti
abbandonasti, e vòlti addietro i passi,
del ritornar ti vanti,
e procedere il chiami.
Al tuo pargoleggiar gl'ingegni tutti,
di cui lor sorte rea padre ti fece,
vanno adulando, ancora
ch'a ludibrio talora
t'abbian fra sé. Non io
con tal vergogna scenderò sotterra;
ma il disprezzo piuttosto che si serra
di te nel petto mio,
mostrato avrò quanto si possa aperto:

Now ruin envelops everything around
where you reside, oh tender bloom, and,
almost as if commiserating with others'
sorrows, you send a perfume of sweetest
scent into the sky, to comfort the arid land.
He who likes to praise the state of man
should come to these slopes, and see how
much loving nature cares for us. And here
he will be able to gauge properly, too,
the strength of the human race, whose cruel
nurse, when it least expects it, with a slight
tremor, can in a moment destroy in part,
and with shocks barely less slight, demolish
just as quickly everything in sight.
Painted on these slopes is mankind's
magnificent and progressive fortunes.

Look here, look at you mirrored here,
proud and foolish age that left the path
which reason, restored, traced forward from
that point, and having turned your steps,
boast of your going backwards and call it
moving ahead. At your prattling, all those
with talent whose bad luck it was to have
you as their father, go singing your praises,
even though, at times, among themselves,
they hold you up to ridicule. I, for one,
will not carry such shame to my grave* but
rather, I'll make sure the scorn I feel for you,
locked in my heart, will have been disclosed
and made public, as much as possible:

---

* The lines below, which follow in an earlier version, were later
deleted by the poet:
  "though I could easily imitate the others,
  and vying with them in singing praises,
  make myself welcome to your ears. . . ."

ben ch'io sappia che obblio
preme chi troppo all'età propria increbbe.
Di questo mal, che teco
mi fia comune, assai finor mi rido.
Libertà vai sognando, e servo a un tempo
vuoi di novo il pensiero,
sol per cui risorgemmo
della barbarie in parte, e per cui solo
si cresce in civiltà, che sola in meglio
guida i pubblici fati.
Così ti spiacque il vero
dell'aspra sorte e del depresso loco
che natura ci die'. Per questo il tergo
vigliaccamente rivolgesti al lume
che il fe' palese: e fuggitivo, appelli
vil chi lui segue, e solo
magnanimo colui
che sé schernendo o gli altri, astuto o folle,
fin sopra gli astri il mortal grado estolle.

Uom di povero stato e membra inferme
che sia dell'alma generoso ed alto,
non chiama sé né stima
ricco d'or né gagliardo,
e di splendida vita o di valente
persona infra la gente
non fa risibil mostra;
ma sé di forza e di tesor mendico
lascia parer senza vergogna, e noma
parlando, apertamente, e di sue cose
fa stima al vero uguale.
Magnanimo animale
non credo io già, ms stolto,
quel che nato a perir, nutrito in pene,
dice, a goder son fatto,
e di fetido orgoglio
empie le carte, eccelse fati e nove

though well I know, oblivion buries
one who was too irksome to his age.
I still laugh to myself no end at this
malady that I must share with you.
You dream freedom, and at the same
time want reason made slave again,
that alone by which we rose once more
from barbarism, in part, and by which
alone civilized life grows, which alone
guides public planning to better things.
So you were displeased with the truth
about your bitter fate and the low place
nature gave us. For this reason you
turned your back cravenly on the light
that made it clear: and, fleeing, call
cowardly he who follows it, and worthy
only he who, mocking himself or
others, cunning or mad, extols this
mortal state beyond the stars.

    A poor man, sick in body, who is
generous and high-minded in spirit,
won't call himself rich or vigorous,
or value such, and doesn't make himself
a public laughing-stock by claiming
an affluent life and a powerful body;
but lets himself be seen, without shame,
destitute of strength and wealth,
and speaking openly about it, and about
his case, honors the truth in the same way.
Hardly a great minded being, in my
opinion, but foolish, one who born
to perish, bred in misery, will say,
I was made to enjoy things, and fills
pages with his rotten pride, promising
here on earth exalted destinies and new

felicità, quali il ciel tutto ignora,
non pur quest'orbe, promettendo in terra
a popoli che un'onda
di mar commosso, un fiato
d'aura maligna, un sottorraneo crollo
distrugge sì, che avanza
a gran pena di lor la rimembranza.
Nobil natura è quella
che a sollevar s'ardisce
gli occhi mortali incontra
al comun fato, e che con franca lingua,
nulla al ver detraendo,
confessa il mal che ci fu dato in sorte,
e il basso stato e frale;
quella che grande e forte
mostra sé nel soffrir, né gli odii e l'ire
fraterne, ancor più gravi
d'ogni altro danno, accresce
alle miserie sue, l'uomo incolpando
del suo dolor, ma dà la colpa a quella
che veramente è rea, che de' mortali
madre è di parto e di voler matrigna.
Costei chiama inimica; e incontro a questa
congiunta esser pensando,
siccome è il vero, ed ordinata in pria
l'umana compagnia,
tutti fra sé confederati estima
gli uomini, e tutti abbraccia
con vero amor, porgendo
valida e pronta ed aspettando aita
negli alterni perigli a nelle angosce
della guerra comune. Ed alle offese
dell'uomo armar la destra, e laccio porre
al vicino ed inciampo,
stolto crede così qual fôra in campo
cinto d'oste contraria, in sul più vivo
incalzar degli assalti,

joys unknown not only to heaven but to
this orb as well, to populations
that angry seas, a breath of tainted air,
a tremor underground can so utterly
destroy that only with great difficulty
will memory of them survive.
A noble nature is one that dares
raise mortal eyes to meet our
common fate, and who, freely,
in no way detracting from the truth,
acknowledges the wrong dealt us
by chance, our low and frail condition;
one who shows himself in suffering
great-minded and strong, nor does
he add to his woes fraternal hatreds
and anger, the worst of ills, by
blaming man for his suffering,
but puts the blame on her who
really is the guilty one, who is birth
mother of mortals, and step-mother
in intent. She he calls the enemy;
and recalling, for it's true, the human
company to be joined together
and organized against her from
the start, he views all men as allies
among themselves, and all he
embraces with true love, offering
immediate and tangible assistance,
expecting the same, in the shifting
dangers and sorrows of their
common war. And thinks it foolish
to take up arms against the wrongs
dealt man, to set a noose or snare
for his neighbor, as when on the
battlefield, surrounded by opposing
ranks, in the midst of the fiercest attacks,

gl'inimici obbliando, acerbe gare
imprender con gli amici,
e sparger fuga e fulminar col brando
infra i propri guerrieri.
Così fatti pensieri
quando fien, come fûr, palesi al volgo,
e quello'orror che primo
contra l'empia natura
strinse i mortali in social catena,
fia ricondotto in parte
da verace saper, l'onesto e il retto
conversar cittadino,
e giustizia e pietade, altra radice
avranno allor che non superbe fole,
ove fondata probità del volgo
così star suole in piede
quale star può quel ch'ha in error la sede.

   Sovente in queste rive,
che, desolate, a bruno
veste il flutto indurato, e par che ondeggi,
seggo la notte; e su la mesta landa
in purissimo azzurro
veggo dall'alto fiammeggiar le stelle,
cui di lontan fa specchio
il mare, e tutto di scintille in giro
per lo vòto seren brillare il mondo.
E poi che gli occhi a quelle luci appunto,
ch'a lor sembrano un punto,
e sono immense, in guisa
che un punto a petto a lor son terra e mare
veracemente; a cui
l'uomo non pur, ma questo
globo ove l'uomo è nulla,
sconosciuto è del tutto; e quando miro
quegli ancor più senz'alcun fin remoti
nodi quasi di stelle

142

forgetting the enemy, he were to engage
in bitter contest with one's allies
and brandish his sword among his own
soldiers and force them to scatter.
When such thoughts become clear,
as they were to everyone, once,
and that horror which first drove
mortals together in social bond
against pitiless nature is recaptured
to some extent by true knowledge,
then honest and proper civil exchange,
and justice and mercy, will have roots
other than the pretentious fables
on which the common man's virtue
is founded and so made to stay
on its feet, if anything can
stay up that's grounded in error.

   Often, I sit at night on these
desolate slopes, which the hardened
flow clothes in black and seems to
billow, and above the sorrowful waste,
against a purest blue, I see the stars
burn, which, in the distance,
the sea mirrors back, and the whole
world lit up with sparks turning
in the serene expanse. Then as I fix
my eyes on those lights, that seem
to them tiny dots and in fact are
immense, so that a point from there
is, in reality, land and sea;
where not only man but this globe
also on which he is nothing
are totally unknown; and when
I see those still more distant
seemingly endless clusters of stars,

ch'a noi paion qual nebbia, a cui non l'uomo
e non la terra sol, ma tutte in uno,
del numero infinite e della mole,
con l'aureo sole insiem, le nostre stelle
o sono ignote, o così paion come
esso alla terra, un punto
di luce nebulosa; al pensier mio
che sembri allora, o prole
dell'uomo? E rimembrando
il tuo stato quaggiù, di cui fa segno
il suol ch'io premo; e poi dall'altra parte,
che te signora e fine
credi tu data al Tutto, e quante volte
favoleggiar ti piacque, in questo oscuro
granel di sabbia, il qual di terra ha nome,
per tua cagion, dell'universe cose
scender gli autori, e conversar sovente
co' tuoi piacevolmente, e che i derisi
sogni rinnovellando, ai saggi insulta
fin la presente età, che in conoscenza
ed in civil costume
sembra tutte avanzar; qual moto allora,
mortal prole infelice, o qual pensiero
verso te finalmente il cor m'assale?
Non so se il riso o la pietà prevale.

Come d'arbor cadendo un picciol pomo,
cui là nel tardo autunno
maturità senz'altra forza atterra,
d'un popol di formiche i dolci alberghi,
cavati in molle gleba
con grande lavoro, e l'opre
e le richezze che adunate a prova
con lungo affaticar l'assidua gente
avea provvidamente al tempo estivo,
schiaccia, diserta e copre
in un punto; così d'alto piombando,

that appear to us as fog, to which not only
man and the earth but the infinite number
of stars, the universe, including the golden
sun, all as one, our stars are either unknown,
or else appear as they to earth, a point
of cloudy light; what then do you seem
like to my mind, oh progeny of man?
And recalling your condition here below,
to which the ground I tread bears witness;
and then, on the other hand, how you
think yourself put here to be lord and end
of All, and the many times you indulged
in telling stories about the authors of
universal things coming down for your sake
to this obscure speck of sand we call
the earth, and talk pleasantly with your
kind often, and how reviving derided
fantasies even the present age, which seems
so far above all others in knowledge
and civil discipline, insults the wise;
what feeling, then, oh wretched progeny
of mortals, what thoughts toward you
does my heart force on me, in the end?
I don't know if laughter or pity prevails.

   As a small apple, falling late in
autumn from its tree, brought down
by nothing other than its own ripeness,
in a second crushes, lays waste and
covers the precious shelters of a whole
nation of ants, scooped out of the soft
earth with great effort, and all their
work, and the riches diligently
gathered in the summer against later
need by the industrious workers;
so too, plummeting from up high,

dall' utero tonante
scagliata al ciel profondo,
di ceneri e di pomici e di sassi
notte e ruina, infusa
di bollenti ruscelli,
o pel montano fianco
furiosa tra l'erba
di liquefatti massi
e di metalli e d'infocata arena
scendendo immensa piena,
le cittadi che il mar là su l'estremo
lido aspergea, confuse
e infranse e ricoperse
in pochi istanti: onde su quelle or pasce
la capra, e città nove
sorgon dall'altra banda, a cui sgabello
son le sepolte, e le prostrate mura
l'arduo monte al suo piè quasi calpesta.
Non ha natura al seme
dell'uom più stima o cura
che alla formica: e se più rara in quello
che nell'altra è la strage,
non avvien ciò d'altronde
fuor che l'uom sue prosapie ha men feconde.

    Ben mille ed ottocento
anni varcâr poi che sparîro, oppressi
dall'ignea forza, i popolati seggi,
e il villanello intento
ai vigneti, che a stento in questi campi
nutre la morte zolla e incenerita,
ancor leva lo sguardo
sospettoso alla vetta
fatal, che nulla mai fatta più mite
ancor siede tremenda, ancor minaccia
a lui strage ed ai figli ed agli averi
lor poverelli. E spesso

out of the thundering womb, night
and destruction infused with boiling
streams of ashes and rocks
and hailstones hurled into the
deep sky, or moving down the side
of the mountain at furious speed
through the grass, a huge mass of
molten metals, scorched sand, rushing
down, brought chaos, destroyed
and covered over, in a few seconds
the cities the sea lapped on the
farthest shore; so that goats graze
there now, and new cities rise
nearby, for which those buried
serve as platorm, and at its base,
the unyielding mountain seems
to trample on the fallen walls.
Nature has no more care or concern
for man's seed than for the ant;
and if such disaster is less frequent
in the one than in the other, that
happens only because man
is less prolific in his breeding.

   More than eighteen hundred years
have passed since those teeming
places disappeared under the fiery
onslaught, and still the poor peasant
tending his vineyards, which grow
with difficulty in the dead scorched
turf, raises his apprehensive gaze
to the lethal peak that, made no
whit kinder, still looms awesome,
still threatens disaster for him and
for his children, and for their meager
belongings, poor people. And often

il meschino, in sul tetto
dell'ostel villereccio, alla vagante
aura giacendo tutta notte insonne
e balzando più volte, esplora il corso
del temuto bollor, che si riversa
dall'inesausto grembo
su l'arenoso dorso, a cui riluce
di Capri la marina
e di Napoli il porto e Mergellina.
E se appressar lo vede, o se nel cupo
del domestico pozzo ode mai l'acqua
fervente gorgogliar, desta i figliuoli,
desta la moglie in fretta, e via, con quanto
di lor cose rapir posson, fuggendo,
vede lontan l'usato
suo nido, e il picciol campo,
che gli fu dalla fame unico schermo,
preda al flutto rovente,
che crepitando giunge, e inesorato
durabilmente sovra quei si spiega.
Torna al celeste raggio
dopo l'antica obblivïon l'estinta
Pompei, come sepolto
scheletro, cui di terra
avarizia o pietà rende all'aperto;
e dal deserto foro
diritto infra le file
dei mozzi colonnati il peregrino
lunge contempla il bipartito giogo
e la cresta fumante,
che alla sparsa ruina ancor minaccia.
E nel'orror della secreta notte
per li vacui teatri,
per li templi deformi e per le rotte
case, ove i parti il pipistrello asconde,
come sinistra face
che per vòti palagi atra s'aggiri,

the poor wretch lying awake all night
in the shifting breeze, on the roof
of his humble dwelling, and jumping up
many times, checks the course of the
feared boiling that spills from the
inexhaustible womb on to the sandy
slopes, and is mirrored in the waters
off Capri, in Mergellina and the port
of Naples. And if he sees it moving close,
or should he ever hear the water
rumbling to a boil down deep in his well,
he hurries to wake up his children,
wake up his wife, and off they go,
with as many of their things as they
can snatch, fleeing, sees from a distance
the familiar hut, and the tiny field
that served as his only shield against
hunger, fall prey to the boiling flood
that crackling, arrives, and relentless,
unyielding, covers them over.
After age-long oblivion, extinct Pompeii
comes to light again, like a buried
skeleton, which the earth gives up
out of greed or pity; and from
the deserted forum straight down
between the lines of broken columns,
the visitor, from a distance,
contemplates the split peak and the
smoldering crater that still threaten
the scattered ruins.
And in the horror of the hidden night,
the glow of the deadly lava races
through gutted theaters, through ruined
temples and through collapsed houses,
where the bat hides her new-born,
like an evil torch that winds its way

corre il baglior della funerea lava,
che di lontan per l'ombre
rosseggia e i lochi introno intorno tinge.
Così dell'uomo ignara e dell'etadi
ch'ei chiama antiche, e del seguir che fanno
dopo gli avi i nepoti,
sta natura ognor verde, anzi procede
per sì lungo cammino
che sembra star. Caggiono i regni intanto,
passan genti e linguaggi: ella nol vede:
e l'uom d'eternità s'arroga il vanto.

    E tu, lenta ginestra,
che di selve odorate
queste campagne dispogliate adorni,
anche tu presto alla crudel possanza
soccomberai del sotterraneo foco,
che ritornando al loco
già noto, stenderà l'avaro lembo
su tue molli foreste. E piegherai
sotto il fascio mortal non renitente
il tuo capo innocente:
ma non piegato insino allora indarno
codardamente supplicando innanzi
al futuro oppressor; ma non eretto
con forsennato orgoglio inver le stelle,
né sul deserto, dove
e la sede e i natali
non per voler ma per fortuna avesti;
ma più saggia, ma tanto
meno inferma dell'uomo, quanto le frali
tue stirpe non credesti
o dal fato o da te fatte immortali.

through empty mansions, that
flisckers among distant shadows
and coming closer, closer,
reddens the area all around.
And so, oblivious of man and all
those ages he calls ancient,
and of the coming of new generations
following the older, nature always stays
young, in fact moves through the long
journey in such a way, she seems
to stand still. Meanwhile, empires
come and go, nations and languages
vanish: she sees it not: and man
arrogantly lays claim to eternity for himself.

And you, supple broom, that beautify
these stripped fields with fragrant groves,
you too will soon fall under the cruel force
of the subterranean fire that, turning
into an already familiar path, will stretch
its greedy boundaries over your pliant
forests. And, you will bend your innocent
head under the mortal burden,
without struggle; but not bent so low
as to seem cowardly begging, in vain,
the oppressor soon coming; but not reach
in foolish pride toward the stars,
or this desert, where not by choice
but chance you had your birth and
have your place; but wiser, but much
less weak than man, since you never
believed your delicate shoots, through
fate's doing or yours, to be immortal.

___

COMMENTARY

Nothing gives more impressive proof of man's greatness and the power of the human intellect, the breadth and nobility of man's spirit, than the fact that he can understand and grasp fully his insignificant role. When he considers the plurality of worlds and feels himself an infinitesimal part of a sphere that is only a part of an infinite system of galaxies, and is stunned by the thought of his insignificance and almost loses himself in that profound and intense contemplation, becoming almost part of the vast void, disoriented in that incomprehensible extension of existence, at that moment with that thought he gives the most convincing proof possible of his nobility, his strength, the great capacity of his mind, which, though enclosed in such an insignificant small being, has come to grasp things so far above his nature and is able tp hold and contain with his thought the immensity of existence and all things.

(Pensieri, V, 8/12/1823)

Nature and the eternal order of things in no way are meant for the happiness of men or animals. The opposite is true. Neither is their own nature or being directed toward it. A being with sensibilities is by nature a suffering being, an essentially suffering part of the universe. Because they exist and perpetuate the species, men like to say that they are a necessary part of the great chain of being, of the order and existence of this universe — which means of course that their misfortunes have a purpose in it, since their existence is nothing but misfortune inasmuch as it is essentially suffering.

(Pensieri, VII, 4/9/1825)

Civilization propagates itself naturally, seeks new conquests, can't stay still or remain within certain given limits, particularly with respect to new areas and it will be that way so long as there are beings who can be civilized and included in the great body of civilization, in the great alliance of intelligent beings against nature and things devoid of intelligence.

(Pensieri, VII, 4/13/1827)

152

My philosophy not only does *not* lead to misanthropy (as some superficial critics believe and accuse it of being) but in fact excludes the possibility of misanthropy since by nature it cures, destroys that irritation, that hatred (not grasped systematically but real nevertheless) which so many who are not philosophers and who would object to being called or considered misanthropes display towards others — habitually or only on certain occasions — because of the evil, which rightly or wrongly, they (like everyone else) are subjected to. My philosophy holds nature responsible for all this, acquits man completely, turns hate or at least our complaints in the direction of the real source of man's sufferings.

(Pensieri, VII, 1/2/1829)

By virtue of the laws of reproduction and destruction and to preserve the actual state of things in the universe, nature is essentially, regularly, and perpetually the persecutor and mortal enemy of every individual of every species and kind she has brought to light; and she begins to persecute them at that very moment that she produces them.

(Pensieri, VII, 4/11/1829)